ASPECTS OF SAXO-NORMAN LONDON: I

BUILDING AND STREET DEVELOPMENT

NEAR BILLINGSGATE AND CHEAPSIDE

ASPECTS OF SAXO-NORMAN LONDON: I

BUILDING AND STREET DEVELOPMENT

NEAR BILLINGSGATE AND CHEAPSIDE

by Valerie Horsman, Christine Milne and Gustav Milne
with contributions by Patrick Allen

London & Middlesex Archaeological Society
Special Paper 11

Published by the London & Middlesex
Archaeological Society

First published 1988

Typeset and printed by BAS Printers Limited,
Over Wallop, Hampshire

Design and production: Melissa Denny of
Diptych

The cover illustration by John Pearson shows a
reconstruction of a street-scene in Saxo-Norman
London.

ISBN 0 903290 36 7

**The Society is grateful to English
Heritage for a grant towards the
publication of this Special Paper**

CONTENTS

ABSTRACT

This, the first volume of a major re-assessment of the development of Saxo-Norman London, is based on the archaeological evidence from seven sites excavated between 1976 and 1985 in the Billingsgate and Cheapside areas of the City of London. There is little evidence for occupation on any of the sites in the mid-Saxon period when the main focus of the settlement lay to the west of the Roman walled town in the Aldwych-Strand area. All seven sites excavated saw substantial development from the late Saxon period onwards.

In Parts 1 and 2 of this volume, the background to the project and the dating methology are explained, and the results of each excavation summarised. In Parts 3 to 6 the often fragmentary remains of some 50 Saxo-Norman buildings are catalogued, described and discussed.

The detailed study of this sometimes poorly-preserved material has revealed evidence of different building types, traditions and techniques. Three main types of structure are represented and the characteristics and possible functions of each type are considered. The single-storied surface-laid buildings seem to represent the standard domestic building set directly against the street frontage; sunken-floored structures were out-houses or storage sheds usually found in the yard area behind the main buildings, while cellared buildings were a uniquely urban type of structure, in which the sub-surface element was set beneath or behind the principal range.

The wide variety of structural techniques observed include the use of earth-fast posts, staves, wattlework and walls founded on baseplates. The evidence for floors, doors, hearths and ovens is also discussed, and reconstructions of two building-types are proposed in Part 7.

In addition, the excavations throw light on the origin of parts of the street-grid in the City through examination of the streets themselves and the layout of the associated properties. It is suggested in Part 8 that the medieval streets just north of Billingsgate were not all laid out in one phase in the 9th–10th century, but represent a gradual development in which primary and secondary streets can be identified.

Detailed reports on the pottery and other finds from the sites discusssed here can be found in the companion volume, *Aspects of Saxo-Norman London, Volume II: Finds and Environmental Evidence*, edited by Alan Vince.

1: INTRODUCTION

Gustav Milne

The background

On the eve of the establishment of the Museum of London's Department of Urban Archaeology (DUA), it was claimed that: 'The archaeology of Anglo-Saxon London barely exists as an organized field of inquiry... Chance discovery and observation ... has made little impact on the study... partly because Anglo-Saxon buildings were usually of timber rather than stone.. but it is also the result of a tendency to concentrate upon the study of Roman London without an equal regard for the archaeology of the City's subsequent periods... It is only from controlled excavations that information has been recovered regarding the buildings of this period, let alone the development of the Anglo-Saxon City as a whole' (Biddle *et al* 1973, 4.20).

In the eleven controlled excavations of Saxon sites within the walls conducted before 1973, very few domestic buildings were recorded. Two were on the *Financial Times* site near Cannon Street, while fragments of others were observed near Bucklersbury and Addle Street: all of these had sunken floors (Grimes 1968, 155-60). Subsequently, the Museum of London's more intensive programme of excavation and research has greatly increased the knowledge of this period. Evidence for Saxon occupation in the form of buildings, pits, wells and other features has been recorded in excavations in many parts of the City, and, crucially, just outside it. In addition, the associated finds, especially the pottery, have been examined in detail. An important consequence of this is that the dating suggested for Saxon deposits is now more reliable.

Recent study has now shown that the majority of the area within the Roman walls was not occupied by a nucleated urban settlement from the 5th to the 9th centuries. The latest Roman occupation deposits recorded were sealed by an horizon of dark grey silts, presumably representing a change to a more rural economy. There is evidence that some sunken-featured buildings may be associated with this phase of development (see MLK76, p. 23; PEN79 p.33). The silt horizon was sealed and cut by features which can be dated no earlier than the 9th century, and, on several sites, to the 10th or 11th. During the period from the 5th to the 9th centuries, it seems that the main focus of the nucleated settlement lay to the west of the walled City, in the area between the Fleet River and Westminster. The evidence to support this suggestion has been developed at some length by Alan Vince (Vince forthcoming), who suggests that the imminent threat of Viking raids in the late 9th century was the stimulus which brought the townspeople back inside the City walls.

However, recent work has also demonstrated that, north of the waterfront in the intra-mural City, the Saxon ground surface is rarely encountered on controlled excavations, since medieval or post-medieval cellars have usually truncated the archaeological sequences below that level. Only on sites where the basements are exceptionally shallow, (or, even more rarely, non-existent) might these levels be encountered. Even where Saxon deposits are identified, they are invariably cut up by later activity into discrete islands of strata. Waterlogged occupation sites of Saxon or Viking date such as those at Dublin (Murray 1983) or York (Hall 1984), or extensively undisturbed though unwaterlogged sites such as those recorded in Thetford (Davison 1968), Southampton (Brisbane forthcoming) or Rhuddlan (Manley 1987) are neither encountered nor anticipated in London. Nevertheless, it is argued here that the disturbed Saxon levels which have already been recorded in the City do provide a valid sample from which much has been learned about London's development from the 5th to the 12th centuries, late Saxon building techniques in the City, and the layout and subsequent growth of its properties and streets. It must be admitted that the archaeology of Saxon London now exists as an organized field of inquiry.

Publication programme

Four complementary reports dealing with aspects of recent research on Saxo-Norman London have been published or are in preparation. The present book, *Aspects of Saxo-Norman London, Volume I*, confines itself to structural and topographical matters, being principally a description and discussion of buildings recorded on a selection of sites near Billingsgate and Cheapside excavated between 1977 and 1985. The pottery, small finds, coins and environmental material from the occupation levels and pits recorded on those sites are catalogued and discussed in *Aspects of Saxo-Norman London, Volume II*, edited by Alan Vince. That volume also contains a discussion of the crucial implications for the dating, relocation and development of the Saxon settlements in London (Vince 1989). A third report, *The Saxon and Medieval Waterfront of London*, will consider the development of the Saxon harbour and waterfront area, assessing the results of the Billingsgate Lorry Park and New Fresh Wharf sites in particular: those sites will not therefore be considered in any depth in the present volume. A further book, *Medieval Buildings and Property Development in the Area of Cheapside* (Schofield and Allen forthcoming) examines the topographical development of the Cheapside area in detail.

The principles behind the writing of this report, *Aspects of Saxo-Norman London, Volume I*, should be set out. These are simply that a body of data representing recent evidence for Saxon buildings in London should be made readily available, that the general context of the discoveries should be established, that parallels should be drawn and questions posed. This volume does not attempt an exhaustive assessment of late Saxon building techniques in England, neither is it a comprehensive catalogue of all late Saxon buildings in London, since the current excavation programme continues to reveal further examples. Nevertheless, this book attempts to advance present knowledge by widening the foundation on which our understanding of the Saxo-Norman City is based.

The study areas

(Fig 1)

The two study areas have been the focus of considerable attention, with a total of seven controlled excavations and subsequent watching briefs between 1977 and 1985.

BILLINGSGATE AREA

(Figs 1, 2)

One study area lies just north of the Saxon harbour at Billingsgate, but south of the market at Eastcheap, between Botolph Lane in the east and Fish Street Hill in the west. The excavations on the Peninsular House (1979-80), Pudding Lane (1981) and Fish Street Hill (1985) sites are considered in this section. These sites also produced evidence for the development of the Roman harbour which has been published elsewhere (Milne 1982; Bateman and Locker 1982; Bateman and Milne 1983; Milne 1985; Bateman 1986), as well as post-medieval deposits (Milne and Milne 1985; Milne 1986).

CHEAPSIDE AREA

(Figs 1, 12)

The other area lies around Bow Lane and Cheapside on a more inland location on the higher ground on the City's western hill. The excavations assessed in this section are those at Milk Street in 1977 (Roskams 1978; Roskams and Schofield 1978), Watling Court in 1978-9 (Perring 1981, 1982), Well Court in 1979 and Ironmonger Lane in 1980 (Norton 1982). The substantial evidence of Roman occupation recorded on these sites is to be published shortly (Perring and Roskams forthcoming), while later medieval material will be considered in a separate volume (Schofield and Allen forthcoming).

Surface-laid and sunken-floored buildings were found in both study areas, together with a large number of truncated pits and wells. As a result of the study of this material, it is suggested that there is no evidence of significant urban occupation in either area before the mid-late 9th century. From that point onwards, however, there was considerable development. Some evidence for the dating of the earliest streets in the Study Areas is considered in the Excavation Summaries in Part 2 and developed in Part 7, while details of the associated buildings are described in the Building Catalogue in Part 3, discussed in Parts 4, 5, and 6, and reconstructions attempted in Part 7.

Excavation methodology

All these excavations were conducted in advance of the imminent redevelopment of the sites.

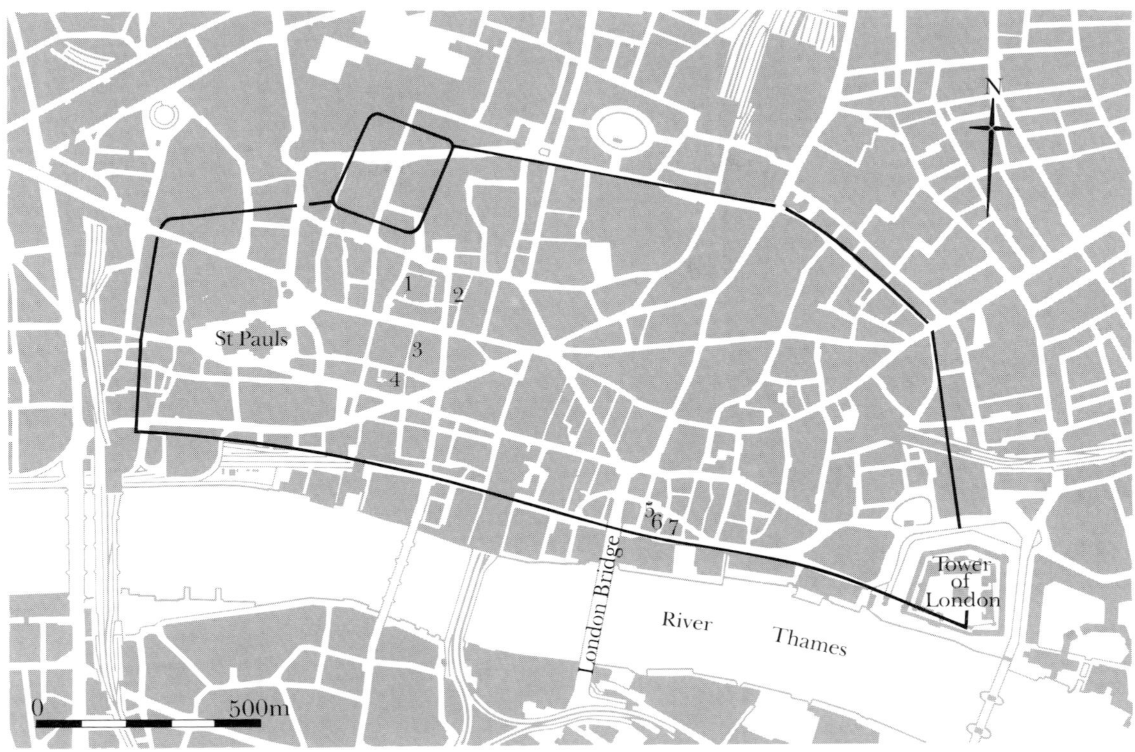

*1. Plan of City streets in 1978, showing the line of the Roman town wall and the locations of the principal archaeological sites discussed in this report: 1. Milk Street (*MLK76*); 2. Ironmonger Lane (*IRO80*); 3. Well Court (*WEL79*); 4. Watling Court (*WAT78*); 5. Fish Street Hill (*FMO85*); 6. Pudding Lane (*PDN81*); 7. Peninsular House (*PEN79*).*

Teams of professional archaeologists with volunteer support were employed to excavate and record the complex stratification in plan, using standard archaeological procedures. Although the sequence in each discrete area was therefore excavated stratigraphically, the contemporary levels in neighbouring areas could not be exposed and excavated at the same time, since it was not possible to know at the time of the excavation which levels of the site were in fact contemporary. In some instances, for example during part of the watching brief and in the trenches cut across Botolph Lane and on PEN79 Area D, the majority of the deposits exposed were only drawn in section.

Post-excavation methodology

Once the controlled excavations had terminated and the contractor's site work had been monitored, archive reports were prepared. The Saxon levels on the Pudding Lane and Peninsular House sites in particular were so badly disturbed that direct stratigraphic correlation between areas was impossible. Nor was it initially possible to establish a basic framework on which the overall site-phasing could be constructed, since no common horizons were positively identifed in adjacent Area sequences. The sequence in each area was therefore written up separately, in stratigraphically-defined blocks termed *Groups* numbered, for example, A1, A2, A3 and so on in the Area A archive report.

A relative chronology was then imposed upon the sequences thus assessed in each trench, based on such indicators as the wear of the floors, or the depth of accumulations. In other words, it was suggested that, by way of a guide, a particular sequence might represent, say, activity over a 50- to 100-year period, rather than over a 10- to 20-year period.

These sequences were then dated absolutely, that is to say at best to the nearest 25 years, after consideration of all the finds and stratigraphic

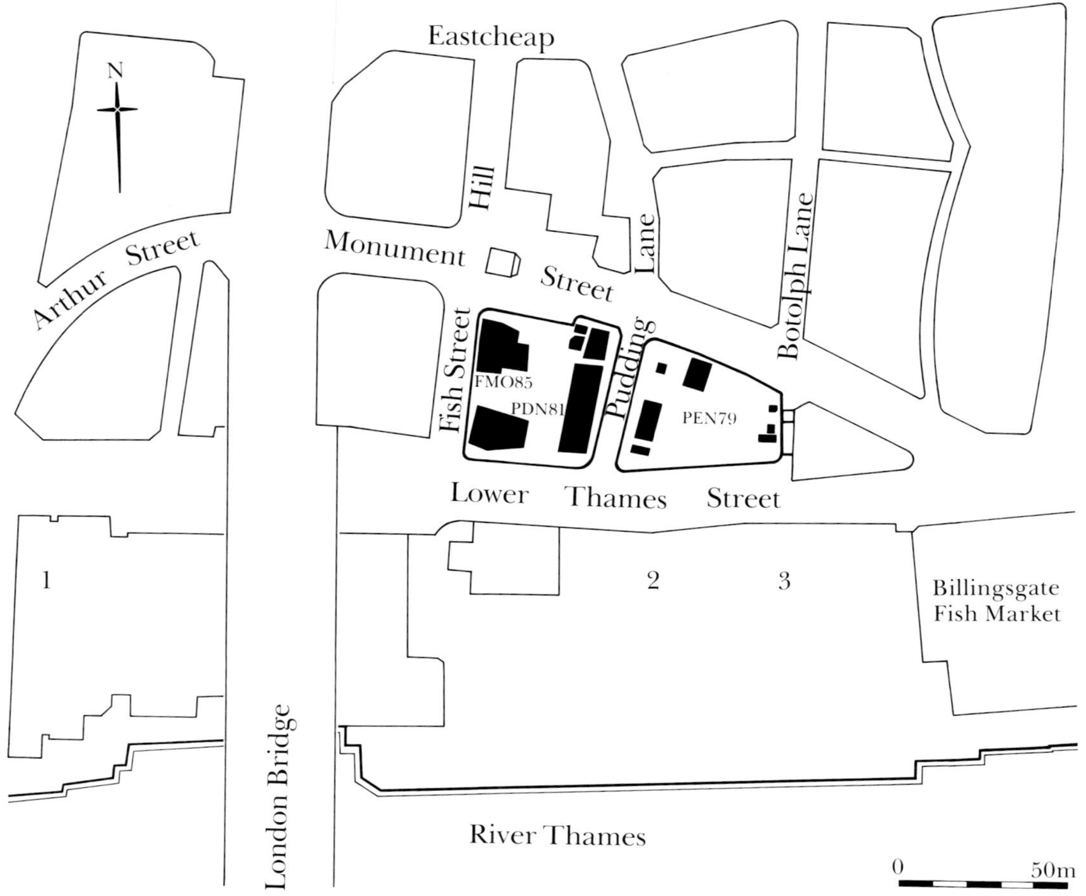

2. Billingsgate study area. The principal sites investigated are shown outlined, and controlled excavations in black: cf Fig 1 (FMO85, PDN81, PEN79). Note that the PEN79 site includes trenches cut across Botolph Lane (Area F) to the east. Other excavations mentioned in the text include: 1. Seal House (SH74); 2. New Fresh Wharf (NFW74) and 3. Billingsgate Lorry Park (BIG82) next to the Billingsgate Fish Market building.

evidence. Deposits or features in different trenches are therefore considered to be contemporary either for stratigraphic reasons or because like assemblages of pottery have been recovered from them: in other words, they belong to the same Ceramic Phase (see below).

At this point, and only at this point, was it possible to integrate the various dated sequences in the otherwise stratigraphically discrete trenches. In this way, the picture of the development of the wider area suggested in this volume was slowly built up. The illustrated reports thus compiled are housed in the Museum of London library, filed by year under their site codes where they may be consulted by written request.

Dating the sequences

(Fig 3)

The dating used in this volume is based on the identification of *Ceramic Phases* (abbreviated to CP1-5 hereafter). These are defined and discussed in detail by Alan Vince in the second volume of this book (Vince forthcoming), and need only be summarised here. Every pottery assemblage recovered from a pit, building or other horizon was assigned to one of the Ceramic Phases depending on the presence, absence and proportion of particular types of pottery in the group. The sequence is based on the examination of assemblages recovered from stratigraphically-related deposits on many sites in the City, but par-

CP	Site ref	Dendro tpq	Coin tpq	date of coin loss	Possible date range
1	Building PEN10	912+			L9-L10th
1	MLK Pit P45	914+			
2					M10-E11th
3	NFW74 Archive 2.4	1014+			
3	BIG82 Archive 4.1	1039-40			E-M11th
4	MLK Pit P55		1017	before 1050	
4	BIG82 Archive 4.4	*c.*1055			
4	NFW74 Archive 3.2	1055+	(probably 1084+)		
4	Building PDN5 PDN 644		1062	before 1066	
4	MLK Pit P41		1074	before 1077	M-L11th
5	PET81 Context 1078		1083	before 1100	
5	BIG82 Archive 4.6 f/s		1080	before 1083	
5	SH74 Pre W1 f/s		1056	before 1100	
5	BIG82 Archive VII	1144–83			
5	SH74 Archive W1	1133–49			E-M 12th
6	SH74 Archive WII	1170			M-L 12th

3. The dating of Ceramic Phases (CP) 1-6 (after Vince, forthcoming).

ticularly the long sequences recorded on the Peninsular House (PEN79) and Pudding Lane (PDN81) sites, as well as the Billingsgate Lorry Park site investigated in 1982-3 (BIG82). The characteristics of each Ceramic Phase are these (see Fig 3 for dating):

Ceramic Phase 1: Late Saxon Shelly alone (LSS)

Ceramic Phase 2: Late Saxon Shelly with Early Medieval Sandy Ware (EMS)

Ceramic Phase 3: Late Saxon Shelly with Early Medieval Sandy and Early Medieval Sand and Shelly Ware (EMSS)

Ceramic Phase 4: absence of Late Saxon Shelly: presence of Early Surrey Coarse Ware (ESUR) and Early Medieval Chalky Ware (EMCH)

Ceramic Phase 5: London-type and Coarse London-type ware (LOND COAR) with locally-produced unglazed greywares (LOGR) alongside types found in previous phase

Although such a broad, relatively-dated sequence can be used to identify contemporary deposits on sites not otherwise startigraphically related, it does not provide absolute dating for the activities represented. However, coins and dendrochronologically-datable material has been found in association with assemblages of CP1, 3, 4 and 5 types, and this information is shown in Fig 3. Some of the deposits in question were excavated on sites considered in this book, for example, MLK76, PEN79 and PDN81. The other sites were at St Peter's Hill to the south of St Paul's Cathedral (PET81), where deposits associated with a late Saxon street were recorded, and New Fresh Wharf, Seal House and Billingsgate Lorry Park (NFW74, SH74, BIG82), where a sequence of waterfront structures dating from the Roman period to the 15th century was recorded (Fig 2).

Obviously, archaeologists dating pits by the pottery found in them need to address such problems as are posed by residual material in the assemblages. Earlier pottery derived from the upcast of the initial digging of the pit could be introduced when the pit is backfilled. Conversely, later material may be dumped into a pit as compensation after its backfill material had compacted and subsided, but such levels may be hard to identify if the top of the pit is truncated. Clearly, allowance must be made for such factors, initially by a rigorous stratigraphic appraisal of the context from which the assemblage was derived.

For these and several other reasons, the date-ranges currently applied to the Ceramic Phases overlap, and may well be refined in the future. Nevertheless, activity associated with CP1-3 can now all be argued as being of pre-Conquest date. In the crucial period of London's development up to the end of the 11th century, four consecutive phases can now be distinguished. The identification and broad dating of the Ceramic Phases therefore marks a major step forward for archaeologists attempting to establish the chronology of Saxon development in London.

2: EXCAVATION SUMMARIES

The purpose of these summaries is twofold: to set the excavated buildings in their topographical and chronological context, and to present the evidence for the dating of the associated streets. This last subject is discussed further below, and also in Part 8, while more detailed descriptions of the better-preserved building fragments are given in Part 3. The summaries presented here are of necessity brief, since the Saxo-Norman levels were rarely deeply-stratified. The majority of features recorded were pits, of which often only the truncated base survived, and these are not here described at any length. The pit numbering system used in the individual site summaries below is the one used in *Aspects of Saxo-Norman London, Volume II*, which considers the relevant finds in detail. Most of the pits would have been some 2m deep; some had been wattle-lined, some were sub-circular in plan, others square. However, the principal concerns in this section of the book are the position of the pits in relation to street frontages and contemporary buildings, and whatever dating evidence can be recovered from their fills. The significance of pits and pit alignments for the study of tenement development in the Cheapside area is reported in a separate study (Schofield and Allen forthcoming).

Dating the streets

At both Bow Lane and Botolph Lane the actual street metalling itself was recorded and dated (Figs 6, 18, 107, 108). The evidence is based on the assumption that the date at which buildings are built up against a street frontage will reflect the date by which the street itself had been established. On these sites, surface-laid buildings occupied the street frontages contemporaneously with, or very soon after, the establishment of the new street. The rubbish pits and wells associated with such developments are usually found outside and to the rear of the contemporary buildings. Pottery from the pits or from the buildings may therefore be used to date the development of the frontage, and thus provide a date by which the street itself must have been established.

Unfortunately, on the majority of the sites considered here, the Saxon ground surface had been truncated, and it was not possible to record the earliest surface-laid buildings on a particular frontage. However, the bases of pits containing datable material often survived below the general level of truncation, and the distribution of such pits in relation to the street frontage is of considerable significance to this study. Although the direct evidence for the position of the earliest surface-laid buildings has not always survived, it is possible to show at which period, and where, the more deeply-cut contemporary pits were and were not dug. A concentration of pits was sometimes seen to lie beyond, and to contrast with, a truncated but unpitted zone parallel to a street and extending some 5 to 10m back from it. Such an unpitted zone is interpreted as representing the area beneath surface-laid buildings initially built up against the frontage but subsequently truncated. The date of the material from the pits which lie outside such a zone is therefore advanced as the date when the contemporary buildings were occupied, the frontage developed, and the line of the street established. Obviously, such an interpretation cannot be afforded the same weight as more direct evidence, but, given the absence of the latter, merits serious consideration.

On another cautionary note, it is accepted that once laid out, the line of a particular street could deviate. Indeed, there is direct archaeological evidence that the eastern side of Bow Lane has moved westwards since its inception. Again, it is quite possible that some of the streets were initially laid out and used as back lanes or trackways long before any buildings were erected next to them. Nevertheless, it is maintained that the approach outlined above provides, at the very least, reliable relative dating for the occupation of the new street frontages.

BILLINGSGATE STUDY AREA

(Figs 2, 4, 5)

Peninsular House
TQ 3295 3340 Site Code: PEN79

(Figs 6, 7)

A five-month excavation during the winter of 1979-80 was supervised by Gustav Milne and funded by Verronworth and Vitiglade. A discontinuous 5m-wide trench was laid out parallel and adjacent to Pudding Lane in the west (Figs 2, 4; Areas A, B, C); sections were also drawn in one of the contractors large trial pits (Area D). Smaller trenches were excavated up against Botolph Lane to the east (Area E), while the opportunity was taken to cut three trenches across Botolph Lane itself (Area F). Evidence of twelve surface-laid late Saxon buildings was recorded, numbered PEN2 to PEN13 in this report, together with the more fragmentary remains of three sunken-floored structures, numbered PEN1, 14 and 15 (see Building Catalogue, pp.33-7).

The three late-Saxon building sequences recorded in adjacent trenches in Area E could not be directly related by obvious stratigraphic connections. The number and nature of the floors and fire levels in each of the sequences were sufficiently different to support the suggestion that three discrete properties had been sampled. The correlation of these separate developments was then attempted, based on a study of the associated pottery and absolute level of the surfaces, together with the matching of some of the horizons of fire debris. Part of the sequence established as a result of that work is shown in Figs 5 and 7, where it is suggested that the southernmost structure, Building PEN8, was the first property established. The properties to the north were developed subsequently. However, not all three properties represented were always built on thereafter, since there was evidence that some remained as open or waste ground for substantial periods after one of the three major fires recorded in this area had destroyed the buildings.

Late 9th-10th century

(Fig 7a & b)

CP1: In most of the areas, the latest Roman floors contained late 4th-century pottery. These levels

4. Composite plan of the Billingsgate study area in the pre-Conquest period. The extent of controlled excavations are marked by a broken line; walls found are shown black and conjectured walls are hatched. Note the position of buildings (not all contemporary) against the Fish Street Hill and Botolph Lane frontages, suggesting the antiquity of those two streets. Note also the distribution of Saxon pits in the middle of the area, indicating that the Pudding Lane frontages were not as intensively developed in this period (FMO85, PDN81, PEN79).

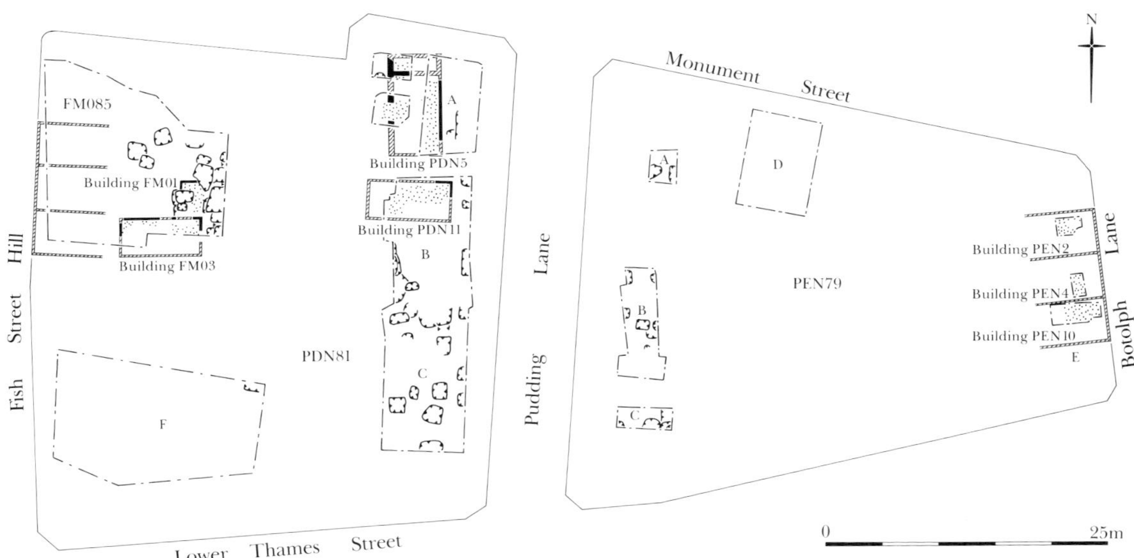

Date	Site codes						
	PEN79			PDN81			FMO85
CP6				PDN10			
CP5				PDN9			
				PDN5			
CP4	PEN14	PEN7		PDN4	PDN8		FMO4
				PDN3	PDN7	PDN11	FMO3
CP3			PEN13	PDN2	PDN6		
		PEN6	PEN12				
CP2		PEN5	PEN11	PDN1			FMO2
	PEN3						
	PEN2	PEN4	PEN10				
			PEN9				
CP1			PEN8				FMO1

5. Sequence diagram showing the relationship of buildings excavated in the Billingsgate study area.

6. Composite section showing the relationship of Buildings PEN *8-* PEN13 *to the earliest surfacing of Botolph Lane. The underlying dumped deposits are shaded (cf Figs 107, 108 (*PEN79*)).*

were sealed by a truncated horizon of dark grey silts at least 300mm thick, perhaps representing dumps of redeposited Roman material. That this material had been disturbed is suggested by the presence of occasional sherds of Saxon pottery (CP1) within it. (Archive Report: PEN79: C8, B10, E5, E9, E14, F1).

An apparently isolated hearth on the western side of the site was associated with CP1 pottery, as was a sequence of surface-laid buildings erected up against the Botolph Lane frontage in the east. The earliest road surface of the Lane itself presumably dates to this phase. Building PEN9 was

7. The development of pre-Conquest properties fronting Botolph Lane. The extent of the controlled excavation is shown with a broken line; walls found are shown in black; conjectured walls are shown hatched; hearths are indicated by heavy stipple PEN79*). a) Building* PEN9 *was erected before properties to the north were developed. b) The three adjacent properties occupied in this phase were destroyed by fire. c) The northern property was rebuilt first (Building* PEN3*) while the two southern properties remained open. d) The southern properties were developed subsequently.*

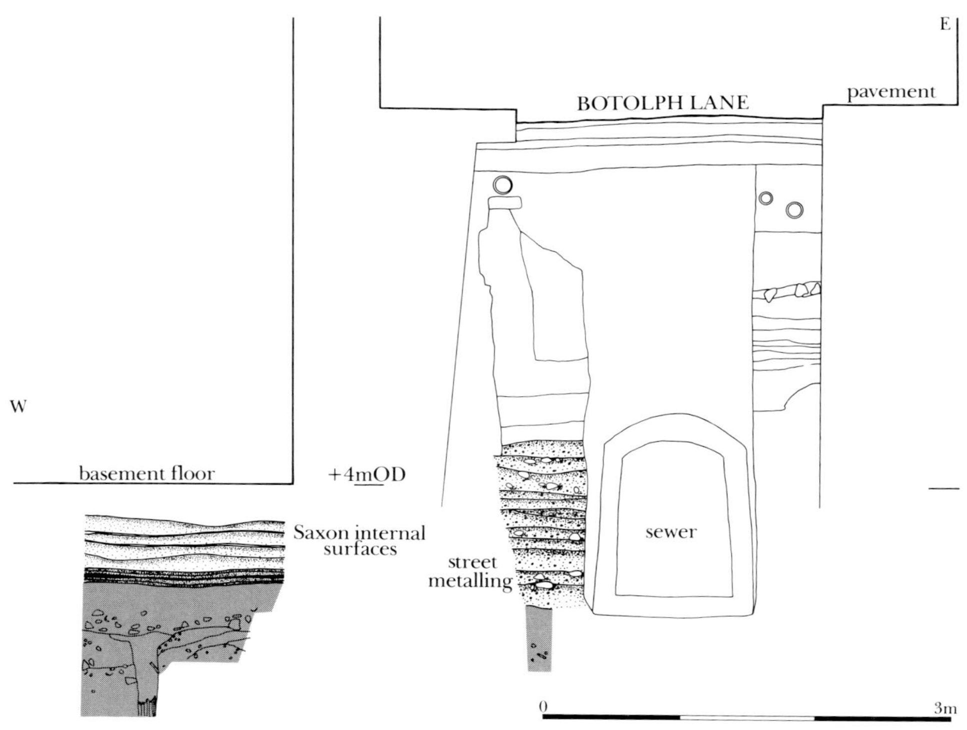

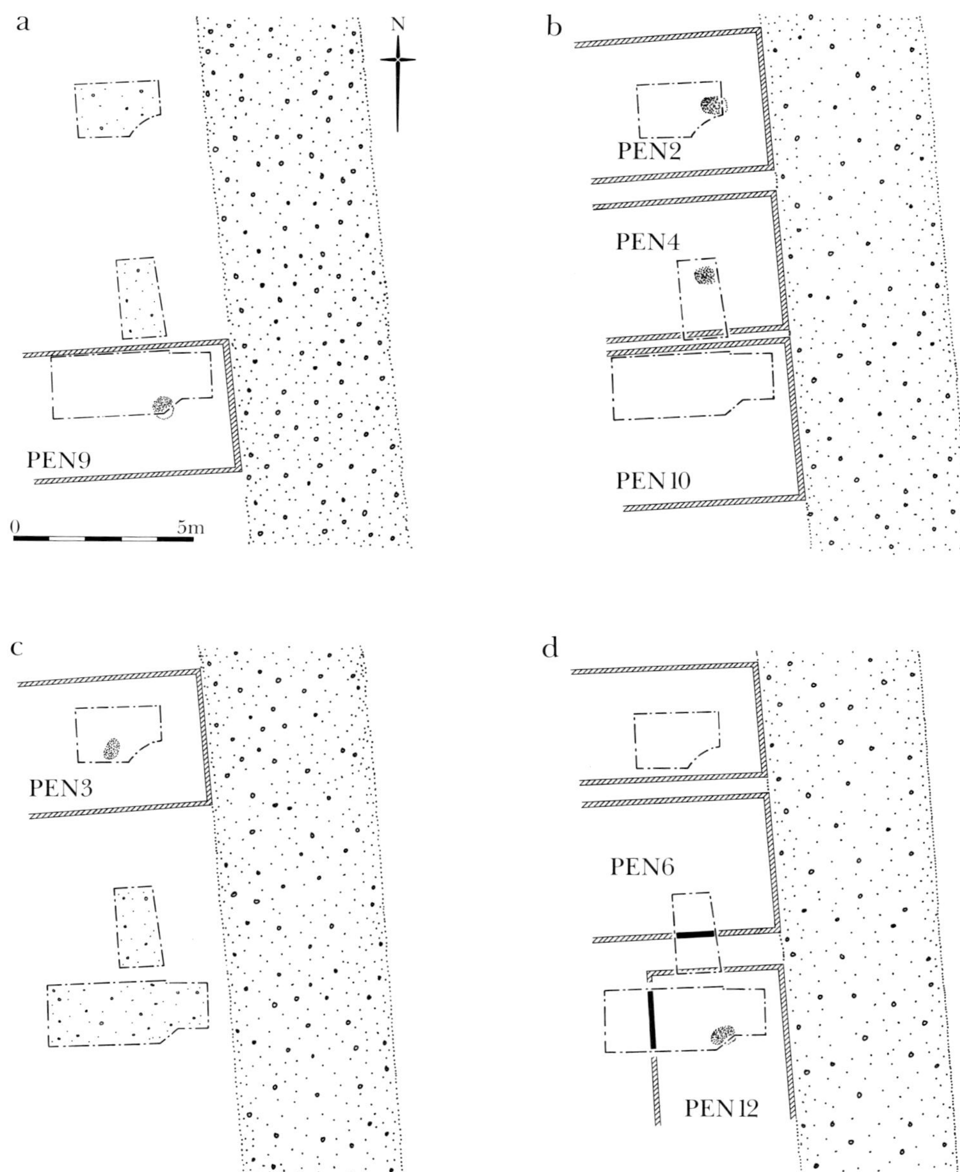
a
N
PEN9
0
5m
b
PEN2
PEN4
PEN10
c
PEN3
d
PEN6
PEN12

superimposed directly over the demolished remains of the earliest building in this area (Building PEN8), and was itself subsequently sealed beneath Building PEN10, which was contemporary with Buildings PEN2 and 4. All three of these buildings were destroyed by fire.

Late 10th-11th century

(Fig 7c & d)

CP2: Surface-laid Building PEN3 was erected up against Botolph Lane, while the two properties to the south remained undeveloped initially. Then Buildings PEN5 and 11 were built, and were subsequently replaced by Buildings PEN6 and PEN12. Pottery of CP2 types was also recovered from pits on the western side of the site.

CP3: Surface-laid Buildings PEN7 and 13 were erected next to Botolph Lane, and CP3 pottery was recovered from a pit on the western side of the site.

CP4: Pottery of CP4 types was associated with sunken-featured Building PEN14 and a pit in west, and also with surface-laid Building PEN7 against Botolph Lane.

12th century

CP5-6: Levels associated with these phases were truncated over most of the site, but in the west at least one pit contained pottery datable to CP5 or later, and another contained pottery of CP6.

Evidence for the establishment of Botolph Lane

(Figs 4, 6, 7)

Examination of the three sections cut across Botolph Lane revealed many common features, although they were over 14m apart. The deposits in the middle of the street had been destroyed by the insertion of a 19th-century brick sewer, and the earlier metalling of Botolph Lane only survived between the sewer and the basement wall. The earliest road surface overlay dumped deposits at a similar level and of a similar nature to those which were sealed by the Buildings PEN2, 4 and 8, which lay just over 1m to the west. Although no pottery was recovered from or directly beneath the street itself (Archive Report PEN79: F1), CP1 pottery was found in association with the occupation levels immediately to the west. Thus the establishment of Botolph Lane and the development of its frontage can be dated to the late 9th - early 10th century.

The record of the road sections shows that the earliest surface incorporated a higher proportion of ragstone and *tegulae* fragments than the upper surfaces, in which there was a corresponding increase in the use of large water-worn flint cobbles (Archive Report PEN79: F2). Layers of grey silt some 100mm thick, representing an accumulation of mud or rubbish, overlay two of the earliest surfaces but did not seal the later more compacted metallings which appeared to be better prepared and maintained than their predecessors. At least three of the more readily-distinguishable surfaces were identifiable on all three sections which were up to 14m apart, spanning at least three tenements. This could suggest that the street was surfaced as a whole rather than in a piecemeal fashion.

Pudding Lane

TQ 3294 8072 Site Code: PDN81

(Figs 2, 4)

Excavations from January to December 1981 were supervised by Gustav Milne, funded by English Property Corporation and National Provident Institution, and the Department of Environment. A trench 8m × 25m long was opened up on the western side of Pudding Lane (Areas A, B, C) and 15m × 8m next to Fish Street Hill (Area F). The site was bounded on its northern edge by Monument Street, a thoroughfare laid out during a 19th-century development which does not relate directly to the medieval street plan.

It now seems that intensive development of the frontages which directly abutted the street beneath Pudding Lane did not begin until the post-Conquest period. Ten Saxon timber buildings and one 12th-century stone-founded building were recorded (Horsman 1983), numbered PDN1 - 11 in this report (see Building Catalogue, pp.37-50).

Late Roman to late 9th-10th century

In Areas B and C the latest Roman occupation levels contained late 4th-century pottery and coins, and were sealed by dark grey silt deposits (Milne 1985, 33, Fig 17e; 138-41, Fig 81e). In Area F, post-medieval and modern basement floors had cut down to 2nd-century levels.

By contrast, in Area A, the north-east part of

the site, a disturbed third-century horizon (Archive Report PDN81 : A1) was sealed beneath laminated silt deposits up to 2m deep. These silts seem to represent the gradual accumulation of water-laid deposits against a Roman masonry terrace wall running east-west across the slope of the hill to the south (Fig 8). The full extent of this pond or marsh was not established. However, it seems that its formation began some time after the blocking of a late Roman revetted watercourse fed by natural springs, which had previously run into the Thames at the foot of the hill. A considerable period of time is presumably represented by this thick horizon, and the almost complete lack of artefacts within the deposit suggests that there was little human activity in the vicinity during this time. This picture is supported by environmental evidence, since the analysis of samples from the water-laid deposits suggests that the surrounding area was waste ground colonised by elder, stinging nettle and dead nettle while the deposits were accumulating (Archive Report PDN81 : A2).

CP1-2 : Sealing the top of the water-laid deposits was a dark grey silt horizon, marked with many root channels (Archive Report PDN81 : A4). Into this level, sunken-floored Building PDN1 was constructed (Fig 9a). A well and 11 pits contained CP1 pottery, while CP2 material was recovered from eight pits.

8. The 5 × 100mm scale stands on the Roman destruction horizon (A) sealed by finely-laminated water-laid silts (B), into which a Pre-Conquest sunken-floored building (C) was cut (PDN81).

11th century

(Fig 9b-d)

CP3: Sunken-featured Building PDN1 was directly replaced by Building PDN2. This was finally backfilled and sealed beneath surface-laid Building PDN3, which was probably contemporary with surface-laid Building PDN6 to the north-west. A well and five pits also contained CP3 pottery. Just to the south, Building PDN11 was erected.

CP4: (Fig 10) The sequence of surface-laid buildings continued in the north of the site with Buildings PDN4, 5, 7 and 8. Sometime after a coin of 1062 had been deposited outside the building close to its eastern wall, Building PDN5 was demolished, and the internal floors and external surfaces sealed beneath a dumped layer. None of these buildings had been erected directly against the Pudding Lane frontage, and they were probably contemporary with four pits. Building PDN11 to the south was backfilled and was cut by three pits.

12th century

(Fig 11)

CP5: In the north of the site, Building PDN8 was destroyed and replaced by Building PDN9, and five pits were dug. Subsequently the building was levelled, and the ground surface raised to form a yard area, sealing the remains of the buildings.

CP6: (Fig 11c) Stone-founded Building PDN10 was constructed, the first structure to have been built up to the Pudding Lane frontage, suggesting that the line of that street must have been established by this time. Another chalk foundation to the south was also contemporary, but the associated levels on the rest of the site had been truncated.

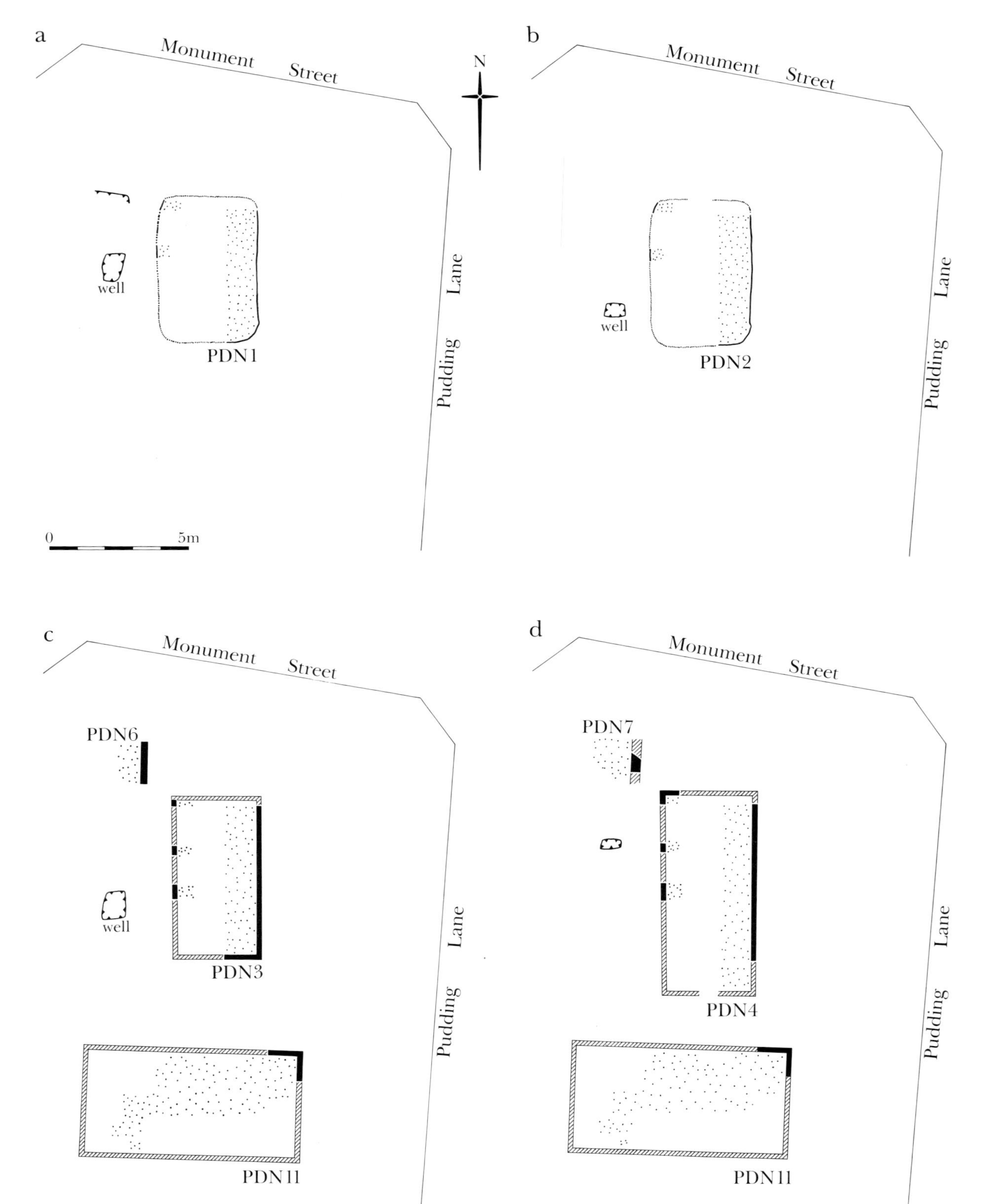
a
Monument Street
N
well
PDN1
Pudding Lane
0
5m
b
Monument Street
well
PDN2
Pudding Lane
c
Monument Street
PDN6
well
PDN3
Pudding Lane
PDN11
d
Monument Street
PDN7
PDN4
Pudding Lane
PDN11

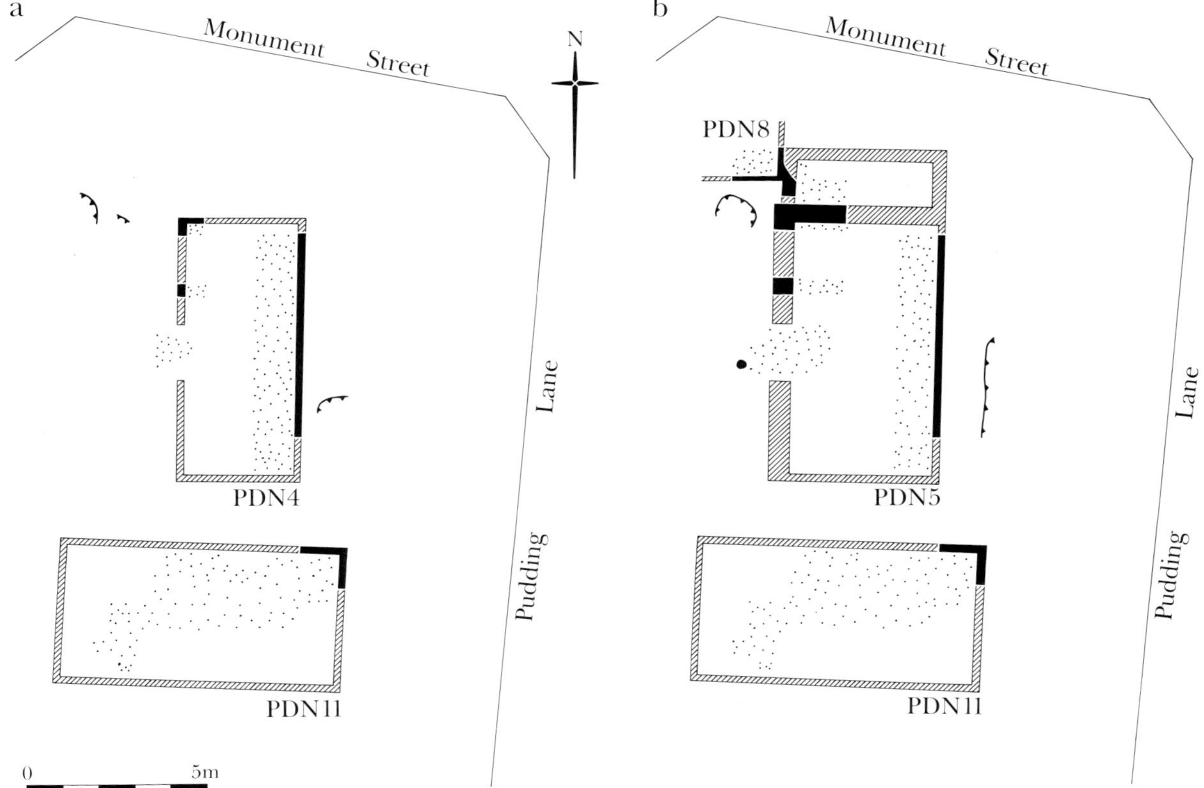

*9. Development at the back of properties which extended to Fish Street Hill to the west, showing change of use from: (a & b) pits and outhouses to (c & d) domestic buildings in the 11th century. The modern street line is shown as on Fig 2. The internal surfaces are shown stippled; walls found are shown black and conjectured wall lines shown hatched (cf Figs 10, 11 (*PDN81*)).*

*10. Later 11th-century development of properties to the east of Fish Street Hill (cf Figs 9, 11 (*PDN81*)).*

Evidence for the establishment of Pudding Lane

(Fig 4)

Since the actual street metallings of Pudding Lane were not exposed and recorded during the recent investigations, the date for its foundation must be argued on indirect evidence. The Saxo-Norman ground surface only survived on the western side of the lane, in Area A. The earliest Saxon buildings recorded there were associated with CP2 pottery, but they did not extend up to the line of what later became the Pudding Lane frontage. Elsewhere on this site, and also on the western side of the Peninsular House site, pits containing pottery of CP1-4 were dug very close to the present-day frontage, demonstrating that those areas were not intensively occupied by buildings at that time. This is in sharp contrast to the Botolph Lane frontage to the east. The only exception to that rule is the isolated sub-surface hearth (CP1) recorded on the PEN79 site (Archive Report PEN79: C8), perhaps associated with an outhouse. The earliest major building which can be argued to have been built up to the Pudding Lane frontage is Building PDN10, which is associated with 12th-century pottery (CP6). The suggestion that both the eastern and western frontages of Pudding Lane were developed in the 12th century is supported by the distribution of pits in the areas immediately adjacent to the street. To the east (PEN79 Areas A, B and C), only two pits contained CP5-6 pottery, while to the west (PDN81 Areas A, B and C) five pits contained CP5 pottery, but none were found with pottery of CP6 or later types.

It therefore seems reasonable to argue that,

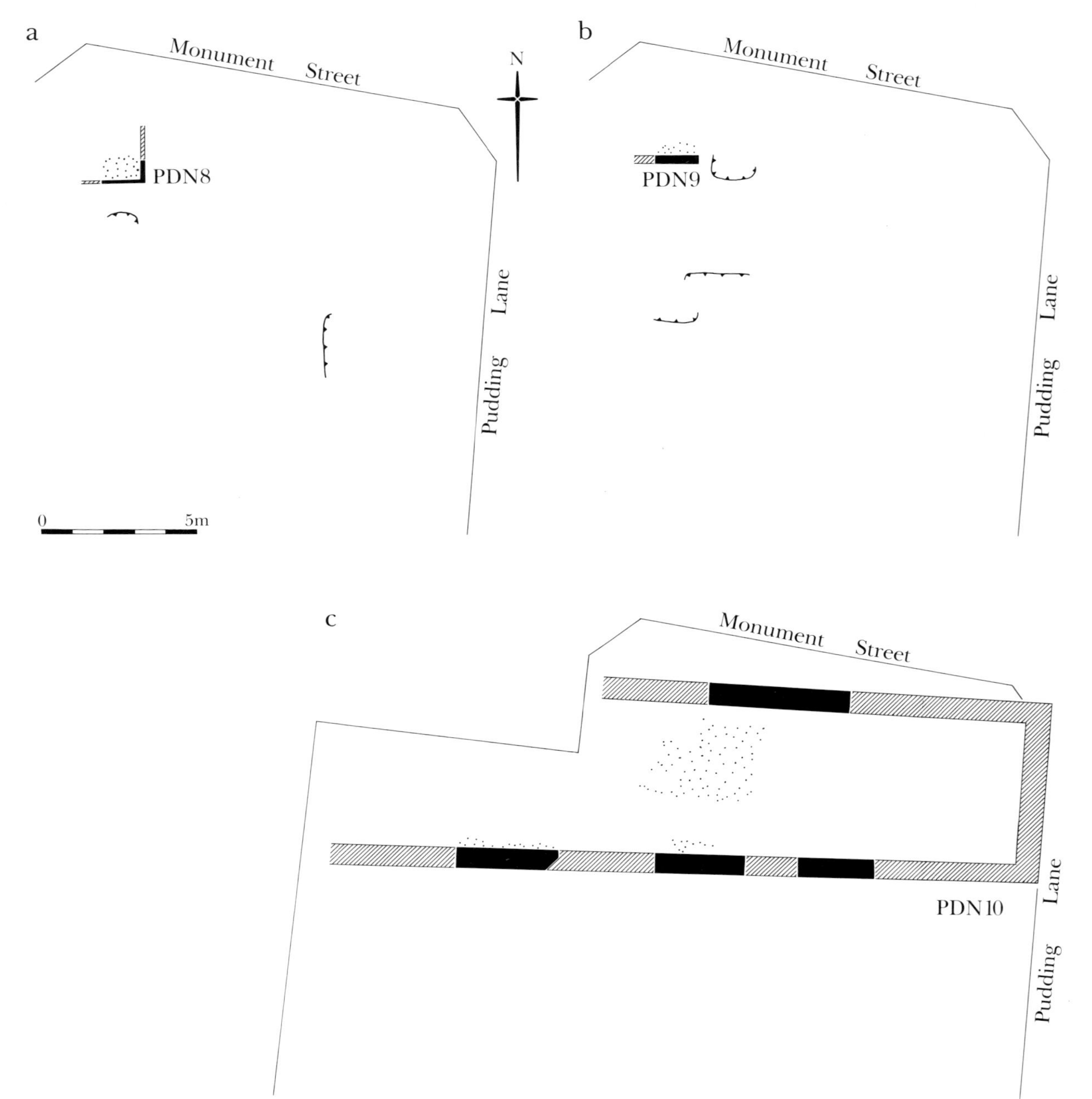

11. 12th-century development of properties to the east of Fish Street Hill (cf Figs 9, 10), showing the (a & b) clearance of 11th-century building and (c) the laying out of Pudding Lane marked by the position of masonry foundations for Building PDN10 (PDN81).

since neither the eastern nor western sides of the lane seem to have been intensively occupied in the pre-Conquest period, the frontages of this lane were not developed until the post-Conquest period, contemporary with Building PDN10. However, it is also suggested that the pits containing pottery of CP1-4 types recorded to east and west of Pudding Lane may well have been at the rear of properties extending to the Fish Street Hill frontage in the west and to the Botolph Lane frontage in the east. If this were the case, then it is quite possible that the predecessor of Pudding Lane was an otherwise undistinguished back lane giving access to the rear of these properties. The 12th-century development of Pudding Lane could therefore be seen, not so much as the laying out of a new road, but the upgrading of such an earlier back lane. This may have been in response to redevelopments in the general area occasioned by the rebuilding of London Bridge from 1176-1209.

Fish Street Hill

TQ 3292 8074 Site Code: FMO85

(Figs 4, 39, 40)

Excavations of an open area 15m by 20m from July to October 1985 were supervised by Nick Bateman, and funded by Speyhawk. The site lay immediately to the west and north of the Pudding Lane excavations (see above), and Fish Street Hill formed the western limit of excavation (Bateman 1986). It now seems that the line of that street was established by the 9th or early 10th century. Although the Saxon ground surface did not survive on this site, 19 pits and two sunken-floored Saxon buildings were recorded, both of which were substantially rebuilt. The building phases are numbered FMO1 to FMO4 in this report (see Building Catalogue, pp.50-52).

Late 9th to 10th century

CP1: The late Roman levels were truncated on this site, but the lower parts of several Saxon pits were recorded, of which two contained pottery of CP1. Both these and all the pits of the succeeding phases were confined to the eastern side of the site, over 5m east of the Fish Street Hill frontage. This implies that the line of that street had been established by this date. The first phase of one of the sunken-floored buildings, FMO1, is also dated to this phase: it was erected some 10m east of the Fish Street Hill frontage.

Late 10th to 11th century

CP2: The sunken-floored Building FMO1 was rebuilt in the same position, FMO2.

CP3: Another sunken-featured building was erected, FMO3. It was aligned east-west and lay some 5m east of the street frontage. Three pits contained CP3 pottery.

CP4: The sunken-featured building was rebuilt in the same position, FMO4. Four pits contained CP4 pottery.

12th century

CP5-6: Five pits contained CP5 pottery, and CP6 pottery was recovered from a further five pits.

Dating evidence for the establishment of Fish Street Hill

Since the Saxon street metallings were not recorded during the recent excavations, the date for the laying out of Fish Street Hill must be determined by considering indirect evidence. Although the Saxon ground surface had been truncated on the eastern side of the street, a number of intrusive features were recorded on the site, demonstrating that the area in general was certainly occupied throughout the pre-Conquest period (CP1-3). Significantly, all these features were confined to an area 5m or more east of the frontage, and it is suggested that the unpitted zone was occupied by surface-laid buildings, the occupants of which would have dug and utilised the pits and other features. The date at which the Fish Street Hill frontage was first developed is therefore argued to be broadly that of the earliest material discarded behind the frontage. Since this is pottery of CP1, it seems that a street on the line of Fish Street Hill had a developed frontage datable to the initial phases of the Saxon re-occupation of the intra-mural area. As such, it would seem that this street was broadly contemporary with Botolph Lane.

CHEAPSIDE STUDY AREA

(Figs 1, 12, 13)

Milk Street

TQ 3235 8124: Site Code: MLK76

(Figs 14, 15 and 16)

Selected areas of this 40m × 30m site near Cheapside were excavated for eight months in 1977,

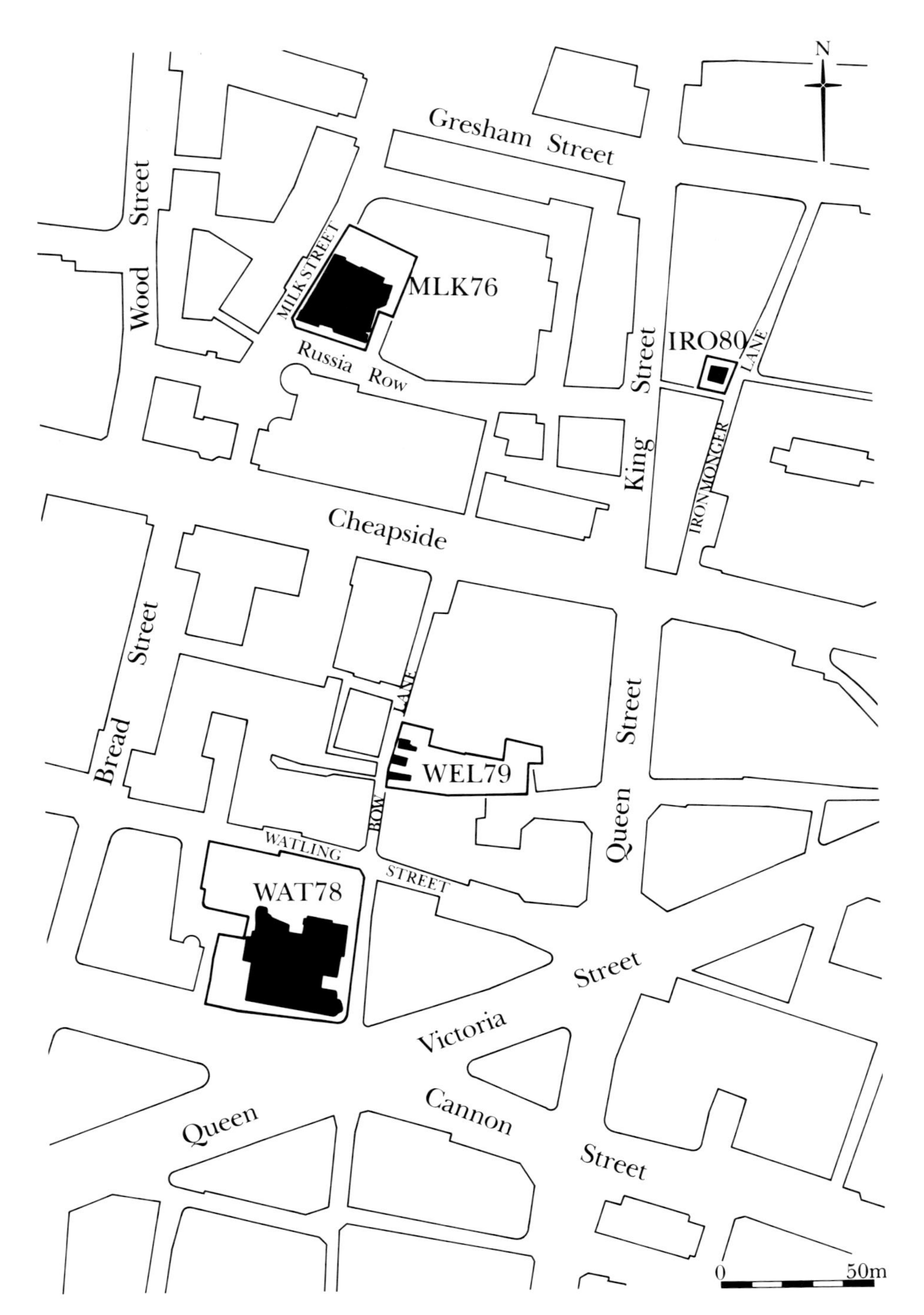
N
Gresham Street
Wood Street
MILK STREET
MLK76
Russia Row
King Street
IRO80
IRONMONGER LANE
Cheapside
Bread Street
LANE
BOW
WEL79
Queen Street
WATLING STREET
WAT78
Victoria Street
Queen
Cannon Street
0
50m

after which a watching brief was mounted. The work, which was supervised by Andrew Boddington, S. P. Roskams and John Schofield, was funded by the Department of Environment and by a Manpower Services Commission Job Creation Programme.

The site lay on the eastern side of Milk Street, which formed the western limit of excavation. The line of this street now seems to have been established by the mid-10th to early 11th century. Evidence of five Saxon timber buildings were recorded, referred to in this report as MLK1 to MLK5 (see Building Catalogue, pp.52-55). The later stone-founded building recorded on this site is described and discussed elsewhere (Schofield and Allen forthcoming).

Late 9th to 10th century

(Figs 14, 41, 42)

CP1: The latest Roman occupation horizon was sealed by dark grey silts *c.*1m thick, from all but the lowest levels of which small quantities of CP1 pottery were recovered. During the watching brief, the sunken-featured Building MLK3 (not illustrated) was observed, apparently sealed beneath these deposits, cutting into the latest Roman occupation level. The form and dating of this building is uncertain: it may even have been associated with Roman or sub-Roman activity.

Sunken-floored Building MLK1 was cut through the western edge of a Roman street which was sealed by dark grey silts and therefore cannot have been in use as a thoroughfare at this time. Ten pits contained CP1 pottery, but formed no clear pattern.

Late 10th-11th century

(Figs 11, 38)

CP2: Building MLK1 was cleared out and reoccupied, and subsequently backfilled. It seems to have been replaced by sunken-featured Building MLK2, which was cut through it and may belong either to this or a succeeding phase. Building MLK4 was constructed up against the Milk Street frontage, extending some 4m eastwards, beyond which were pits and a well. Building MLK5 replaced Building MLK4.

*12. Plan of the Cheapside study area. The principal sites investigated are shown outlined; the extent of controlled excavations in black. (cf Fig 1 (*MLK76, IRO80, WEL79, WAT78*)).*

Date	Site codes								
	MLK76		IRO80	WAT78			WEL79		
CP4				WAT2		WAT3		WEL6	WEL7
CP3			IRO3	WAT1	WAT4			WEL5	
		MLK5							
CP2	MLK2	MLK4	IRO2				WEL3	WEL4	
	MLK1		IRO1					WEL2	
CP1								WEL1	

13. Sequence diagram showing the relationship of buildings excavated in the Cheapside study area.

No pits were dug against the Milk Street frontage in this phase but at least six pits contained CP2 pottery.

CP3-4: (Figs 15, 16) With one exception, no pits were dug within 7m of the street frontage in these phases. The contemporary ground surface had been truncated over most of the site. Seven pits contained CP3 pottery and at least 28 pits contained CP4 pottery.

Evidence for the establishment of Milk Street

Since medieval street metallings were not exposed during the recent excavations, the date for the laying out of Milk Street must be based on indirect evidence. Study of the pottery assemblages recovered from the site has shown that substantial occupation in the general area in the post-Roman period dates from the late 9th-early 10th century onwards (CP1-5). However, the earliest building which might be argued to reflect the development of the Milk Street frontage is Building MLK4 which cannot be dated earlier than the mid-10th century (CP2). However, both this building and the earlier Building MLK1 are aligned north-south, rather than east-west, perhaps suggesting that the major frontage lay to the south rather than to the west in this period. The general alignment of the pit groups in the succeeding phase is, however, quite markedly east-west, perhaps indicating a change in the orientation of the burgage plots.

Evidence from this complex site could therefore be interpreted as suggesting that the primary late Saxon development of the area was focused on the southern frontage (CP1, 2), but that the orientation of these properties changed in the subsequent period, implying that a new frontage had been established in the later 10th and 11th century (CP3, 4), presumably on the western side of the site. Whether or not this interpretation is

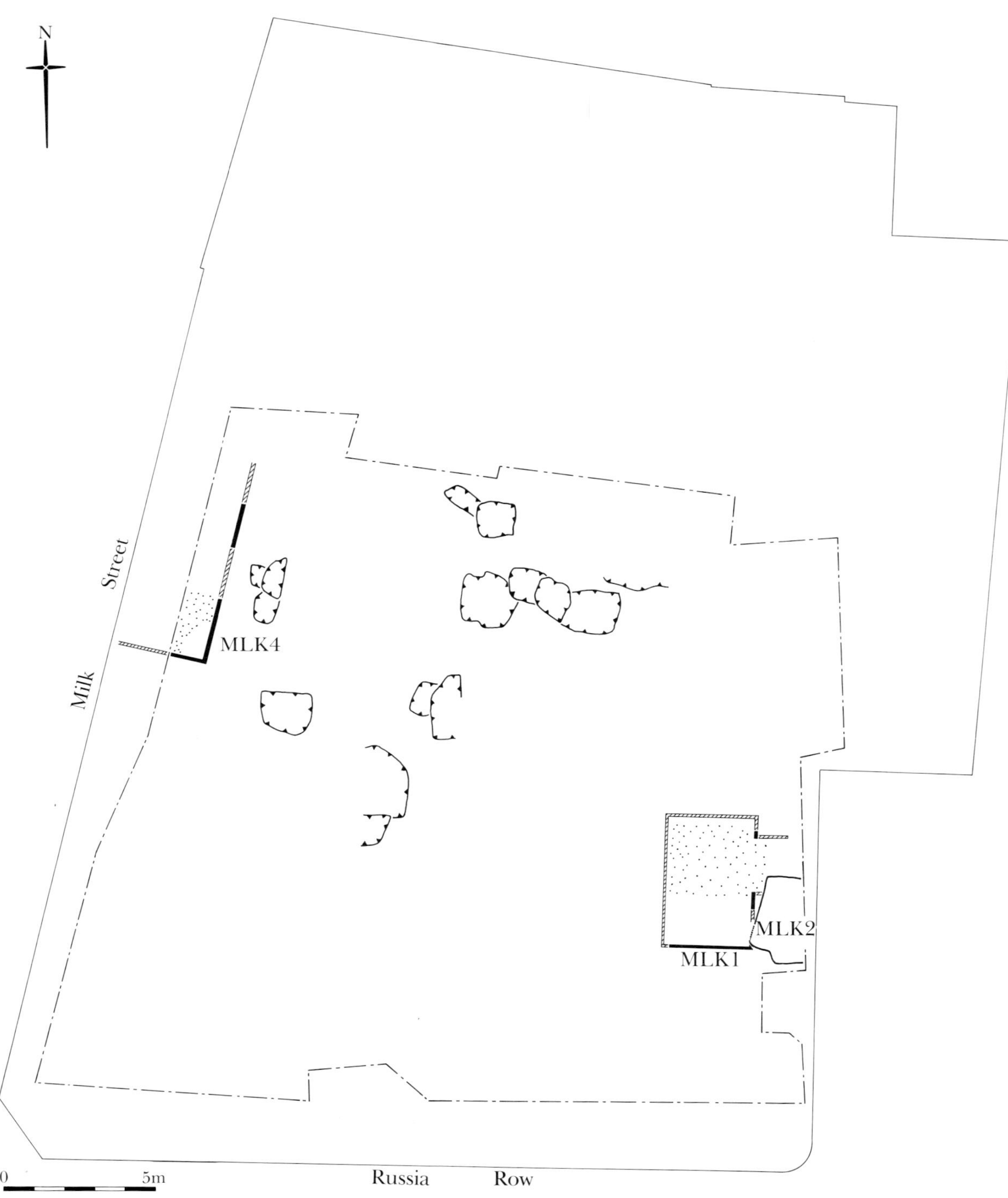

*14. Plan of the Milk Street site showing major pre-Conquest features (*CP 1-2*), with the extent of controlled excavation shown by a broken line (cf Figs 12, 15). Sunken-floored Building* MLK1 *is shown in relation to contemporary pits containing* CP 1-2 *pottery. Note the position of later Building* MLK4 *built up against the Milk Street frontage (*MLK76*).*

15. Plan of pit alignments on the Milk Street site in the 11th century (CP4)*. Note the absence of buildings in this phase (cf Figs 12, 14* (MLK76)*).*

*16. Pit alignments on the Milk Street site, looking west. 10 × 100mm scales (*MLK76*).*

accepted, it can be said that the Milk Street frontage was developed by the 11th century (CP3 or 4), but not before the late 10th century (CP2), although the general area had been occupied before that date (CP1). The development of the Milk Street frontage would therefore seem to be later than that argued for Bow Lane, a street to the south of Cheapside (see below).

Watling Court

TQ 3235 8105: Site Code: WAT78

(Figs 1, 12, 17)

A major excavation from June 1978 to February 1979 was followed by a watching brief on this 40m by 40m site. The work was supervised by Dominic Perring, and funded by the Department of Environment (Perring 1982). The site lay on the western side of Bow Lane close to the junction with a street formerly known as Basing Lane, now part of Cannon Street, to the south. Although the Saxo-Norman ground surface had been truncated over much of the site, the bases of many pits were excavated. In addition, evidence of four large late-Saxon sunken-floored buildings was recorded, referred to in this report as WAT1 to WAT4 (see Building Catalogue pp.56-61). The remains of a 12th-century stone-founded building are discussed elsewhere (Schofield and Allen forthcoming).

Late 9th-10th century

CP1 - 2: Dark grey silts up to 1m thick sealed the latest Roman levels. 19 pits contained CP1 pottery, and were cut into this horizon but most did not extend as far south or east as the street frontages.

11th century

CP3: Sunken-floored Building WAT1 was erected on the Bow Lane frontage. Ten pits contained pottery of CP3 types.

CP4: Building WAT1 replaced by the larger Building WAT2, built 13m back from the street frontage. A third large cellared Building WAT3 was constructed 5m from the present street frontage to the south. Some 6m to the west, cellared Building WAT4 may be contemporary. Some of the 14 pits which contained CP4 pottery were cut through the backfill of these buildings.

12th century

CP5: In the west of the site, a phase of dumping raised the ground surface by between 0.3 and 0.6m, over which brickearth surfaces were laid. 11 pits contained CP5 pottery, and were dug both in this area and in other parts of the site away from the street frontages.

Evidence for the development of Basing Lane

No direct dating evidence for the laying out of Basing Lane (now Cannon Street) was recovered from this excavation. However, pits containing assemblages of CP1 and 2 pottery were recorded, showing that the earliest post-Roman occupation in the general area was of 9th to 10th-century date. The north-south alignment of Building WAT3 suggests that it was associated with a property built up against a street frontage to the south, which implies that the line of Basing Lane had already been established by the 11th century

17. General plan of the eastern half of the Watling Court site, showing the postion of pits containing CP4 *pottery in relation to cellared Buildings* WAT1, WAT2, WAT3 *(cf Fig 12 (*WAT78*)).*

(CP4). However, the notable absence of earlier pits in the southern part of the site directly behind the street frontage is significant. This could suggest that the area was already occupied by surface-laid buildings in the previous phase (CP1-3), the direct evidence for which was unfortunately truncated.

To sum up, it seems that the Basing Lane frontage was almost certainly developed by the mid- to late 11th century (CP4), probably in or by the mid- to late 10th century (CP2-3), and possibly even earlier (CP1). Clearly, more work on the dating of this particular east-west street is required. This is of considerable importance since most of the recent detailed work on the dating of the post-Roman street system has been concentrated on the principal north-south thoroughfares, but it is not clear how large the primary insulae were, or when, how, or if they were sub-divided subsequently.

Well Court

TQ 3238 8108: Site Code: WEL79

(Figs 1, 12)

Excavation of three small 2m × 10m trenches and observations over a wider area of this 20m × 50m site just to the north of Watling Court took place in 1979. The work was supervised by Dominic Perring and funded by the Department of Environment. The western limit of excavation was formed by Bow Lane, the line of which now seems to have been established in the 10th century. Evidence for seven late Saxon timber structures were recorded, referred to as WEL1 to WEL7 in this report (see Building Catalogue pp. 61-64). The remains of a 12th-century stone-founded building also recorded on this site are discussed elsewhere (Schofield and Allen forthcoming).

Late 9th-10th century

(Fig 18)

CP1: A 0.7m thick deposit of dark grey silt sealed the Roman deposits and was cut by sunken-floored Building WEL1, which is thought to pre-date the first two street surfaces. The south-west corner of surface-laid Building WEL2 respected the line of this street, which must therefore have been established by this phase. Unfortunately, none of these features was dated directly, but all are presumably contemporary with CP1 or 2, since they are earlier than Building WEL3. Two pits may be contemporary, since the pottery recovered from them could belong to this or a succeeding phase (CP1-4).

10th-11th century

(Fig 19-20)

CP2: Although pottery from Building WEL3 could belong to CP1, 2 or 3, an associated structure, WEL4, has been dated archaeo-magnetically to (*c*.950–1000). To the east of these buildings, cellared Building WEL7 was probably contemporary but may be as late as CP4.

CP3: No pottery from this phase was recovered, but the deposits representing the disuse of Building WEL3 were sealed layers containing pottery of CP4 types.

CP4: Building WEL3 was replaced first by Building WEL5 and then by Building WEL6, which encroached further onto the eastern edge of the street (Fig 20). Some of the five pits containing CP4 pottery cut through Buildings WEL6 and WEL7.

18. The pre-Conquest street surface exposed on the Well Court site, with a 5 × 100mm scale (WEL79).

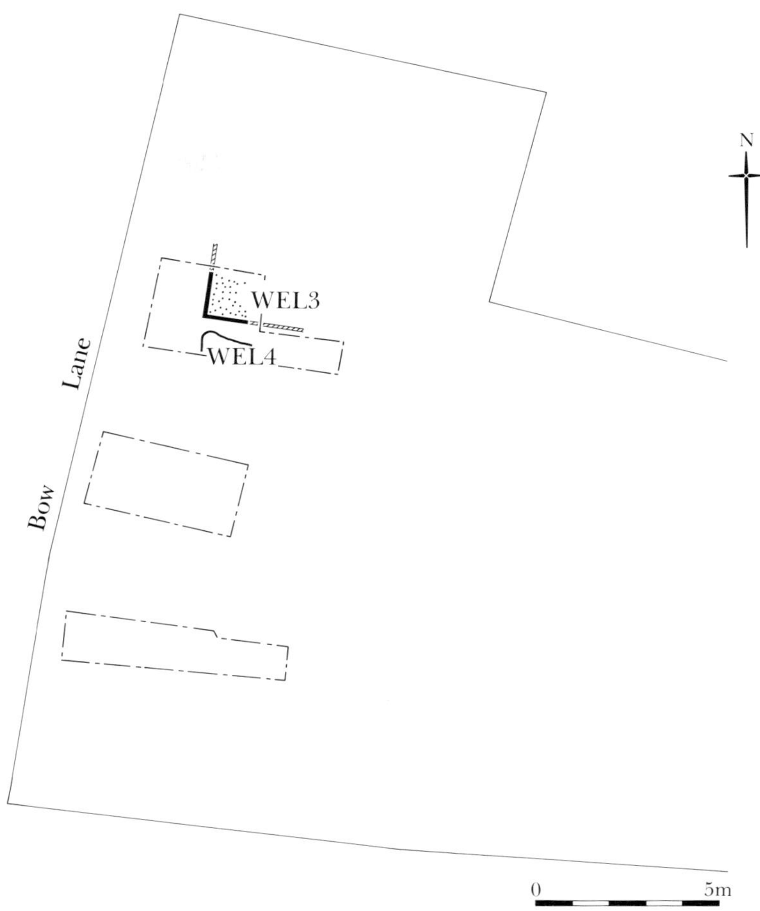

19. Plan of the western half of the Well Court site showing the position of surface-laid Building WEL3 *and sunken Building* WEL4 *(*CP2*), with the Saxon street surface to the west (*WEL79*).*

Evidence for the establishment and development of Bow Lane

(Fig 12)

The eastern edge of the first two metalled surfaces of Bow Lane were exposed on the Well Court site. The earliest surface was roughly paved with re-used Roman ragstone and roof tile bedded in gravel, and had been laid over a thick dark grey silt deposit completely sealing the underlying Roman levels. Unfortunately no pottery was recovered from the street surfaces, but the lane must have been established by the time Building WEL2 was erected, since its south-west corner abutted the eastern edge of the street. The small group of pottery associated with that building could belong to CP1, 2 or 3. No pottery was found with the occupation levels of the succeeding Building WEL3, but the the pottery from the major phases which were stratigraphically later (Buildings WEL5-6) was of CP4 type. The evidence from the Well Court site therefore demonstrated that Bow Lane was laid out substantially before the Conquest, certainly by CP3-4, and in all probability during CP1-2.

The indirect evidence recorded on the Watling Court site does not contradict that conclusion. The position and alignment of Building WAT3 suggests that the western frontage of Bow Lane was being developed by the 11th century, CP3. However, pits containing pottery of CP1 and 2 types were recorded to the west of an unpitted area against the western edge of Bow Lane. Such an area may have been occupied by surface-laid buildings subsequently truncated.

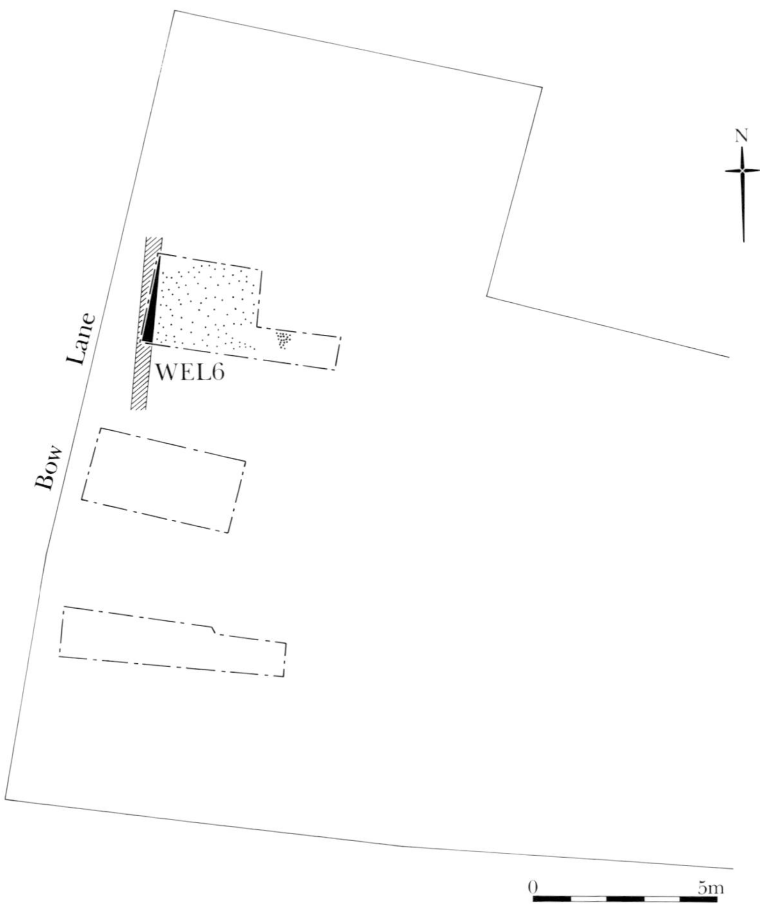

20. Plan of the western half of the Well Court site showing the position of surface-laid Building WEL6 *(*CP4*), which has encroached upon the street surface shown in Fig 19.*

Taken together, the evidence from these two sites on either side of Bow Lane shows that this street was certainly established in the pre-Conquest period by the 11th century (CP3). It would not be unreasonable to suggest a 10th-century date for its foundation (CP2), while the evidence considered here does not discount a late 9th-century origin (CP1). As such, it is possible to argue that Bow Lane was one of the earliest Saxon streets, broadly contemporary with Botoloph Lane and Fish Street Hill in the Billingsgate study area.

Ironmonger Lane

TQ 3238 8108: Site Code: IRO80

(Figs 1, 12, 21)

The four-month excavation of an 8m × 8m area north of Cheapside in 1980 was supervised by Jenny Norton, and funded by Guardian Royal Exchange (Norton 1982). The site lay on the western side of Ironmonger Lane, which formed the eastern limit of excavation. The line of this road now seems to have been established by the early 12th century. Evidence of three late Saxon buildings was recorded, referred to as IRO1 to IRO3 (see Building Catalogue pp.64-65).

Late 9th-10th century

CP1: The latest Roman levels were sealed beneath a 0.5m thick layer of dark grey silt, with the exception of the top of a stone boundary wall and the disturbed uppermost surface of an east-west Roman street. Cutting into that surface was sunken-featured Building IRO1.

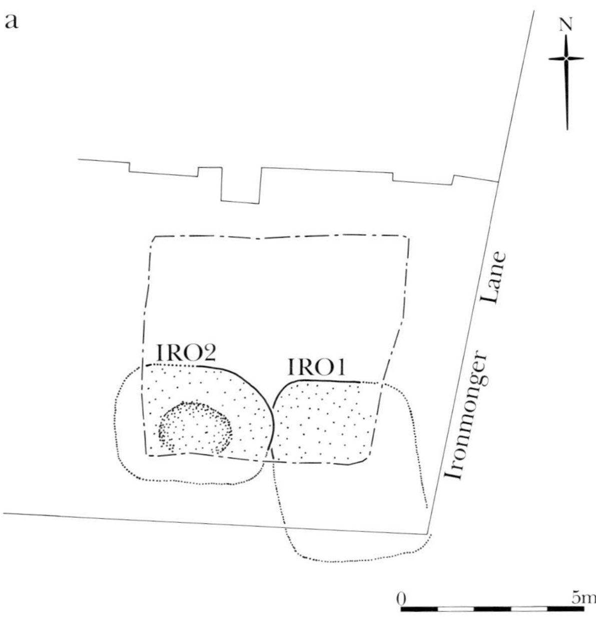

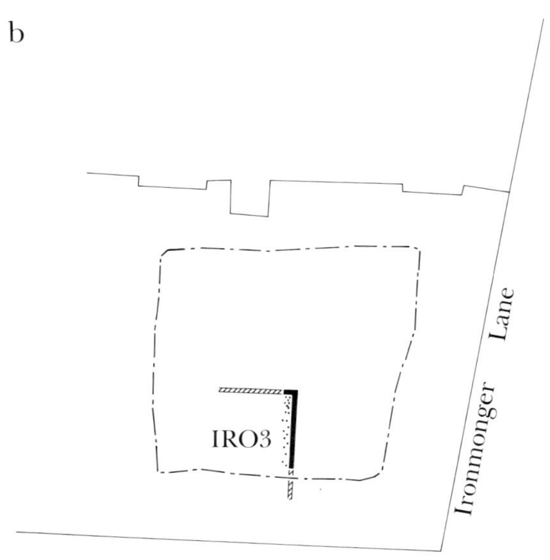

21. Development of properties north of Cheapside, showing (a) change of use from outhouses CP1-2 *to (b) surface-laid buildings,* CP3 *(*IRO80*).*

10th–11th century

CP2: The sunken-featured Building IRO1 was backfilled, and replaced by Building IRO2. The Roman boundary wall was razed, and the whole area levelled. Two pits contained CP2 pottery, while a further five pits contained pottery of CP2-3 types.

CP3: Building IRO3 was constructed in the same position as Building IRO2 but at a higher level, 6m west of the Ironmonger Lane frontage. Gullies and five pits containing CP3 pottery were dug to the north and east of the building.

CP4: Six pits contained CP4 pottery.

12th century

CP5: The four pits containing CP5 pottery were all dug on the western half of the site, respecting a levelled area to the south-east which was presumably associated with a building built against the Ironmonger Lane frontage.

Evidence for the establishment of Ironmonger Lane

The recent investigations produced no direct dating evidence for the laying out of Ironmonger Lane. However, the initial post-Roman phases comprised pits containing pottery of CP1-3 types and structures interpreted as outhouses, features which are usually found in backyard areas rather than along developed street frontages. By contrast, later pits which contained CP5 pottery were concentrated in the western half of the site, which could suggest that the frontage to the east was occupied at that time by surface-laid buildings, the direct evidence of which was truncated. This would imply that the Ironmonger Lane frontage was developed in the post-Conquest period, in or by the 12th century (CP5), and not substantially earlier.

3: TIMBER BUILDINGS CATALOGUE

There are 48 entries in this building catalogue, in which a 'building' is defined as a structure with a fairly complete outline; a structure with one or more wall-lines associated with another feature such as an entrance, floor or hearth, or simply a sequence of internal surfaces sandwiched between identifiable make-up and destruction horizons but where no evidence of walls survived. The recording of an isolated wall-trench or patch of floor is not therefore included here.

In this report the buildings are numbered in a simple numerical sequence for each site, the building numbers being prefaced by the abbreviated site code thus: PEN = Peninsular House, PDN = Pudding Lane, FMO = Fish Street Hill, MLK = Milk Street, WAT = Watling Court, WEL = Well Court, IRO = Ironmonger Lane

The entries have been compiled from sections of the site archive reports written by the following authors: PEN79, Area E—D. Bowler and G. Milne; PDN81, Area A—V. Horsman; PDN81, Area B—C. Guy; FMO85—N. Bateman; WAT78 and WEL79—P. Allen and D. Perring; MLK76—P. Allen; IRO80—J. Norton.

BILLINGSGATE STUDY AREA

Peninsular House (PEN79)

Building PEN1

(not illustrated)

Plan: possible sunken-floored building observed in section only: 0.5m deep: *c.*1m E-W: unknown N-S.

Walls: carbonized fragments of planks laid vertically against W edge may represent timber lining.

Internal features: beaten-earth floor 80mm thick identifed, overlying traces of a possible brickearth surface. Infilled with mixed deposits including fragments of burnt daub and some Roman building material including painted wall plaster.

Dating: probably CP1. Sealed by substantial dumped deposits over which Building PEN2 (CP1) was ultimately laid.

Archive ref: PEN79, Group E4.

Building PEN2

(Fig 7a)

Plan: fragment of surface-laid building, 3m E-W × 1.4m N-S.

Walls: no evidence.

Internal features: 0.4m thick brickearth floor laid directly over rammed surface of substantial grey silt makeup level. Associated in first phase with brickearth hearth slab incorporating solid base of tile, flint and limestone fragments. This feature replaced by an oval basin-shaped oven lined with brickearth, 0.4m long, 0.3m across, 0.4m deep. Scorched brown patina on surface, discoloured red beneath, laid over prepared sand and coarse pebble base.

Area resurfaced with 30mm thick brickearth surface associated with new oven laid over a pebble and brickearth base. This comprised an oval hollow around which was a wattle-strengthened brickearth wall scorched bright red, and a flue to the north incorporating large fragments of Roman roof tile. At least three carbonised superimposed horizontal wattles survived, woven around four vertical members in the west wall. The floor of the basin was blackened and contained a deposit of carbonised grain.

Area resurfaced with 20mm thick brickearth covered with 0.2m thick debris deposit including frequent charcoal, burnt brickearth and daub fragments.

Dating: CP1. Overlies dumped deposits sealing Building PEN1; sealed by Building PEN3 (CP2).

Archive ref: PEN79, Group E6.

Building PEN3

(Fig 7c, 93)

Plan: fragment of surface-laid building, 3m E-W × 1.4m N-S.

Walls: no evidence.

Internal features: 40mm thick beaten-earth surface covered area, associated with three stakeholes, and a hearth/oven feature comprising two brick-earth wall stubs separated by an area discoloured by intense burning in situ from white-pink-red to black. It had a compacted base up to 30mm thick.

At least six major phases of repairs or resurfacing of the floor were recorded, incorporating superimposed floors of beaten-earth and brickearth.

The latest surviving surface was cut by three intrusive features and by the insertion of the 19th-century cellar floor.

Dating: CP2. Directly overlies Building PEN2 (CP1).

Archive ref: PEN79, Group E7.

Building PEN4

(Fig 7b)

Plan: fragment of surface-laid building, 1.6m E-W × 1.7m N-S.

Walls: no evidence.

Internal features: beaten-earth surface laid out over rammed surface of substantial dumps sealing Roman levels. A 10mm thick brickearth slab incorporating tile and ragstone fragments formed the base of a hearth. It had been discoloured dark brown to black, and had been in use with a second surface, which was of brickearth.

The floor was resurfaced with beaten-earth, brickearth and beaten-earth and the hearth slab replaced with a second brickearth slab which had been burnt red-brown. This horizon was sealed by charcoal destruction level.

Dating: CP1. This building was the first of a sequence of structures which sealed Roman levels, but was itself overlain by Building PEN5 (CP2).

Archive ref: PEN79, Group E10.

Building PEN5

(not illustrated)

Plan: fragment of surface-laid building, 1.4m E-W × 1.7m N-S.

Walls: no evidence.

Internal features: 40mm thick brickearth surface to the N of which was sandy gravel spread over which the first of several hearth/oven slabs was laid. To the S was a beaten-earth floor cut by two stakeholes.

The surface was replaced by a mixed deposit; the hearth by the discoloured brickearth base. This horizon was sealed by mixed grey silts cut by a stakehole over which was a third hearth/oven base cut by three stakeholes.

This horizon was sealed by beaten-earth deposit over which a fourth hearth/oven base was laid.

To the south a beaten-earth surface was laid, over which was a fifth hearth/oven base cut by two stakeholes. There was some evidence that this slab was retained within a squared timber frame-work (cf Building PEN11) as a burnt timber was found *in situ* on its S edge and the ashy remnants of a second timber defined the E edge. Sandy mortar represented a sixth hearth/oven base. This horizon was sealed by a deposit of burnt debris 10mm thick.

Dating: CP2. Later than Building PEN4 (CP1); earlier than Building PEN6 (CP2).

Archive ref: PEN79, Group E11.

Building PEN6

(Fig 7d, 87)

Plan: fragment of surface-laid building, 1.2m E-W × 1.7m N-S.

Walls: 1m long fragment of S wall line: flint cobbles and occasional ragstone rubble set in sandy silty gravel bed, at least 0.3m wide, associated with a posthole 0.2m in diameter.

Internal features: beaten-earth floors were cut by

eight stakeholes and resurfaced with a brickearth surface.

This horizon was cut by a 0.2m-wide slot which could represent a bench or similar E-W internal feature laid out parallel to but 0.8m N of the S wall. Although several phases of brickearth floor accumulated to the N of this slot, only one 60mm thick silt deposit accumulated to the S of it, ie beneath the possible bench feature.

Dating: CP2-3. Later than Building PEN5 (CP2); earlier than Building PEN7 (CP4).

Archive ref: PEN79, Group E12.

Building PEN7

(not illustrated)

Plan: fragment of surface-laid building, 1m E-W × 1.4m N-S.

Walls: no evidence.

Internal features: laid over a beaten-earth floor was a 30mm thick brickearth slab discoloured by burning, representing the base of a hearth/oven, which had been replaced after destruction. A second beaten-earth floor was then laid, over which was a third hearth/oven base.

The latter was replaced by a brickearth base and later by a fifth hearth/oven base, which had probably been set within a timber framework, and was cut by three stakeholes. A substantial grey silt horizon sealed these features, presumably marking the demolition of that building. Its upper surface may have served as a beaten-earth floor, but it was sealed by a series of deposits which had all the characteristics of internal floor surfaces.

Dating: CP4. Later than Building PEN6 (CP2-3).

Archive ref: PEN79, Group E13.

Building PEN8

(see Fig 6)

Plan: fragment of surface-laid buidling, 2.7m E-W × 2.1m N-S.

Walls: four postholes for posts *c*.80mm in diameter aligned *c*.E-W may mark part of a N wall. However, the associated internal floor extends N of this alignment, suggesting that the postholes may represent aisle or ridge post supports.

Internal features: Over a rammed surface of 0.5m thick grey silt deposits was a yellow coarse sand with patches of brickearth. It was confined to the W of the area. To the E was a group of ten stakeholes, at least four of which were aligned N-S, perhaps representing a wattle partition or similar internal feature.

These features were sealed by a deposit of brown silt containing much wood fibre, which suggests that the PEN8 building was demolished, and was not burnt down.

Dating: CP1. Earlier than Building PEN9 (CP1).

Archive ref: PEN79, Group E14.

Building PEN9

(Fig 7a)

Plan: fragment of surface-laid buidling, 2.6m E-W × 1.4m N-S.

Walls: posthole containing a post 60mm in diameter may represent part of N wall line.

Internal features: most of the area covered by a beaten earth floor which was cut by a shallow depression, 1.1m long by 0.3m wide, filled by a compacted slab of scorched brickearth, forming a hearth base.

The area was resurfaced with brickearth, the W part of which was cut by a scatter of 11 stakeholes, and the hearth was replaced with brickearth slab. This horizon sealed by layer of silt and wood fragments suggesting that the building was demolished, rather than burnt down.

Dating: CP1. Later than Building PEN8 (CP1); earlier than Building PEN10 (CP1).

Archive ref: PEN79, Group E15.

Building PEN10

(Fig 7b)

Plan: fragment of surface-laid building, 2.7m E-W × 1.4m N-S.

Walls: no evidence in first phase, but see gulley feature and posthole in later phase, which may relate to the N wall.

Internal features: A beaten-earth floor up to 200mm thick covered much of the area, over which was an ashy brickearth slab, some 20mm thick by 1m by 0.5m, cut by five stakeholes. Subsequently, a much-repaired brickearth surface overlay a grey brown silt makeup level. That horizon was in turn sealed by a brickearth floor, over the eastern part of which was a brickearth floor. This was cut by three stakeholes and, on its northern edge, by a posthole. Extending eastwards from that was another feature, a 0.7m length of plank-lined gulley, *c.*150mm wide and up to 110mm deep.

It is suggested that this building was destroyed by fire, since the uppermost horizon just described was covered by a layer of charcoal and ash. The property was not rebuilt immediately, but was left as open ground for a substantial period of time, after which Building PEN11 was erected.

Dating: CP1. Later than Building PEN9 (CP1) earlier than Building PEN11 (CP2).

Archive ref: PEN79, Group E16.

Building PEN11

(see Figs 6, 94, 96)

Plan: fragment of surface-laid building, 2.7m E-W × 1.7m N-S.

Walls: no evidence.

Internal features: the deposits representing external activity which overlay the remains of Building PEN10 were sealed beneath a gravel spread. A linear impression on its northern edge may mark the position of a bench or similar feature laid out parallel to the N wall. Into the gravel surface six stakeholes were cut. One of these was sealed by the timber framework enclosing an area, 1.2m E-W by at least 1.3m N-S, of well-compacted sands and gravels, into the middle of which a circular basin 0.4m across and *c.*50mm deep was cut. This was filled with ashy brickearth with evidence for *in situ* burning. A substantial oven is clearly represented, while the accumulation of ash layers on its western side suggests that its mouth lay on that side.

The eastern half of the area was sealed beneath grey silt the western half beneath sandy brickearth. Much of this horizon, although not the oven itself, was covered by grey silt, which was cut by 11 stakeholes. This building seems to have been destroyed by the fire represented by the ash layer.

Dating: CP2. Later than Building PEN10 (CP1); earlier than Building PEN12 (CP2).

Archive ref: PEN79, Group E11.

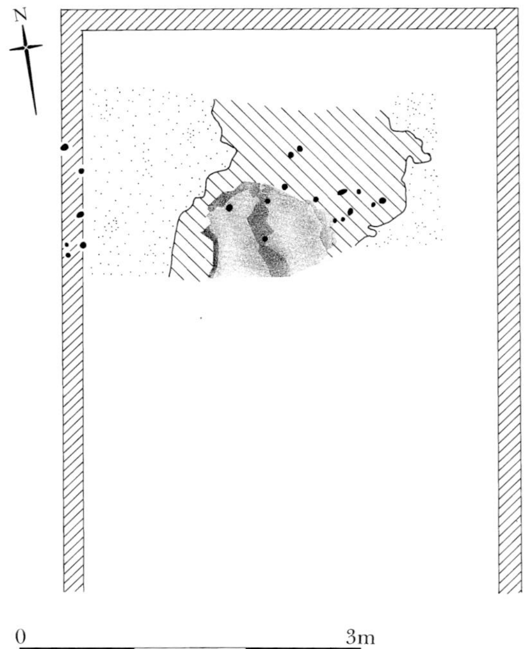

22. Plan of Building PEN12, *with conjectured wall line. The oven is shown shaded; stakeholes are shown in black and the brickearth floor hatched.*

Building PEN12

(Figs 7d, 22, 95)

Plan: fragment of surface-laid buidling, 4m E-W × 1.8m N-S.

Walls: a group of five stakeholes in a *c.*N-S line probably mark the W wall line, since they separate an internal area to the E from an external area to the W. The stakes probably supported a wattle wall.

Internal features: the ballast and timber platform of the earlier Building PEN11 was cut by a shallow basin, 0.9m in diameter and 85mm deep, lined with brickearth and filled with stones and tile fragments. Around this was laid a brickearth surface, which was scorched black in an arc around the stone-filled reservoir, reflecting the outline of the superstructure of the oven itself. Within this arc, the compacted brickearth had been burnt bright orange. A number of stakeholes representing structures in use with the oven and also support for its superstructure were recorded. There was evidence for a contemporary sequence of beaten-earth and brickearth floor repairs.

The latest horizon was sealed by a deposit of ash representing burning thatch, which significantly extended just west of the stakehole line thought to mark the W wall line.

Dating: CP2. Later than Building PEN11 (CP2); earlier than Building PEN13 (CP3).

Archive ref: PEN79, Group E19.

Building PEN13

(see Fig 6)

Plan: fragment of surface-laid buidling, 3.5m E-W × 1.6m N-S.

Walls: a N-S line of six stakeholes (a replacement of the N-S line described for the Building PEN6) marked the line of the W wall of the building.

Internal features: a layer of grey silt and midden material was dumped over the ash marking the destruction of Building PEN12, over which was evidence of a worn, patched floor and a brickearth hearth slab discoloured orange by *in situ* burning. The latest levels associated with this building were disturbed by modern activity.

Dating: CP3. Later than Building PEN12 (CP2).

Archive ref: PEN79, Group E21.

Building PEN14

(not illustrated)

Plan: fragmentary and truncated remains of possible sunken-floored building at least 1m E-W by 1m N-S.

Walls: no evidence

Internal features: two patchy brickearth surfaces up to 20mm thick were separated by a thin layer of grey silt with small shell fragments at *c.* +3.5m OD, at least 0.3m lower than the estimated height of the truncated contemporary ground surface. The S edge of the later brickearth floor lapped over the edge of a shallow oval pit 0.3m deep and 0.8m by 1m across. This suggests that the pit was open while the floor was in use.

Dating: CP4. Overlies or cuts into horizon of dark grey silt containing late Roman pottery; cut by pits (CP4).

Archive ref: PEN79, Group C8.

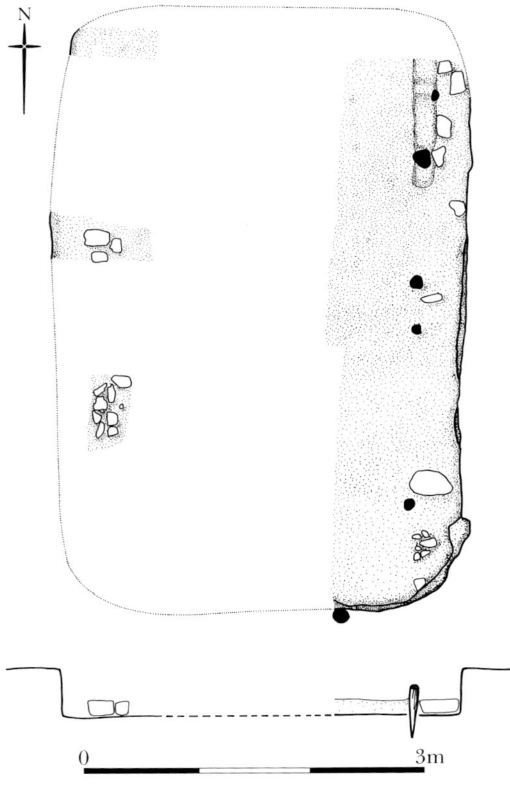

23. Plan and reconstructed profile of sunken-floored Building PDN1. The padstones supporting the baseplate retained by stakes are shown in black; the internal floor surface is stippled and the conjectured line of the construction pit dotted (cf Figs 24, 98).

Pudding Lane (PDN81)

Building PDN1

(Figs 9a, 23)

Plan: a sub-rectangular sunken-floored building *c.*5.5m N-S × *c.*3.7m E-W. Set 0.41m into the underlying water-laid deposits. The surface of these deposits formed a gradual slope dropping from N to S.

Walls: the walls, probably wooden, were supported on timber baseplates. The E and W walls were carried on rows of levelled ragstones and reused Roman tiles laid in the bottom of the sunken area. Inside the E alignment of padstones, five stakes protruding no more than 100mm above the contemporary surface were preserved as vertical voids: the northernmost of these stakes were set in a shallow rectangular feature. Evidence of the S and N wall foundations was destroyed during the erection of later buildings PDN2 and PDN3 respectively.

Although the superstructure itself had been dismantled and removed, the surviving remains clearly indicate the use of timber baseplates supporting a wooden framework. There was evidence that mud cladding at least 1.1m high was piled against the outer face of the walls.

Immediately to the S of the building, the impression of a deeply driven square stake, 0.11m × 0.13m, angled towards the building, may have contained a roof support or formed part of an external revetment to the mud cladding.

Internal features: four shallow slots cut into the base of the sunken area, parallel to its E and S sides, may have contained several planks set horizontally on edge, acting as supports for a wooden floor, subsequently removed. The slots were overlain by a compacted beaten earth floor from which a pair of blacksmith's tongs (see Vince forthcoming,) were recovered.

Subsidence in its SE corner prompted the dismantling of the entire building. Its wooden components were carefully removed, presumably for reuse.

Dating: CP2. The building was set into accumulated water-laid deposits which sealed 3rd or 4th century Roman levels. It was immediately succeeded by Building PDN2 (CP3).

Archive ref: PDN81, Group A7.

Building PDN2

(Figs 9b, 24)

Plan: sub-rectangular sunken-floored building c.5.5m N-S × c.3.7m E-W laid out on the site of Building PDN1 reusing the same wall-lines.

Walls: probably wooden walls carried on timber baseplates. The E and W walls were supported on rows of levelled padstones which had previously supported the walls of the earlier Building PDN1. The S wall rested on a similar row of levelled reused Roman tiles raised on a platform of ash and charcoal, probably compensating for earlier subsidence. Inside the S wall-line the void of at least one deeply-driven stake protruding approx. 0.12m above the contemporary internal surface

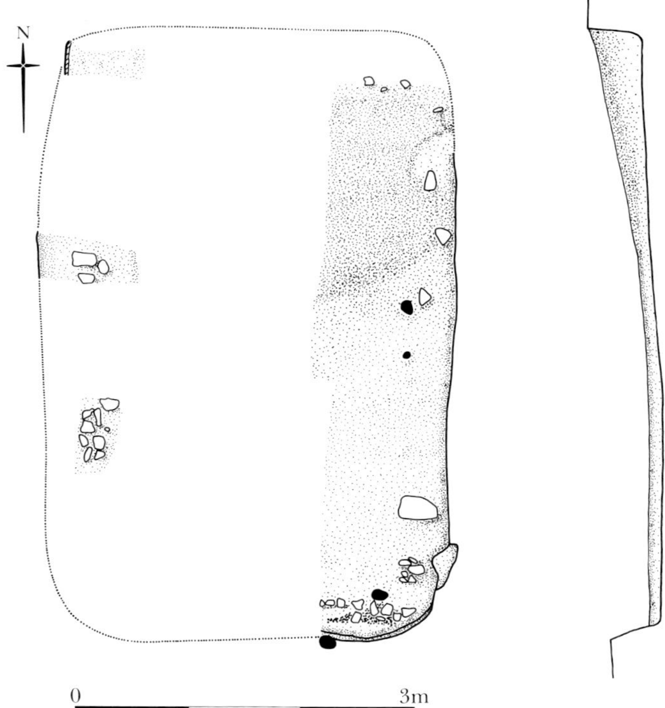

24. Plan and profile of sunken-floored Building PDN2. Note the ramp leading to the entrance at ground level to the north (cf Fig 23).

was preserved. It, together with two of the stakes which had previously revetted the E wall of the earlier Building PDN1, retained the SE corner against the sides of the sunken area. These carefully prepared footings imply the use of timber baseplates supporting a wooden superstructure. There was evidence that mud cladding, at least 1.1m high, was piled against the exterior of the building. The stake acting as external roof support or revetment to the S wall was retained.

Entrance: earthen ramp rising to ground level at the N end of the building.

Internal features: a very compact beaten earth surface was laid over the latest floor of the earlier Building PDN1, incorporating the entrance ramp. In the NW corner this floor was overlain by successive thin lenses of occupation debris over which a preparatory makeup layer was laid for a later beaten earth surfacing. The impression of a slightly curved plank, perhaps representing part of a wooden lining, separated this surface from the edge of the sunken area.

The sunken area was deliberately backfilled after the removal of the superstructure. The infill included large lumps of clearly laminated waterlaid deposit, previously preserved within the external mud cladding. A levelled silt platform was then laid out over the infilled sunken area, preparatory to the construction of Building PDN3.

Dating: CP3. Laid out over Building PDN1 (CP2); sealed by Building PDN3 (CP3).

Archive ref: PDN81, Group A7.

Building PDN3

(Figs 9c, 25, 26)

First phase

Plan: rectangular surface-laid building, *c*.6.4m N-S × *c*.3.2m E-W, terraced at its N end where the internal surface was up to 0.5m below the contemporary external surface. It reused the same E-W and N wall-lines as the earlier Buildings PDN1 and PDN2, but extended further to to the S.

Walls: timber baseplates probably supporting stave walls. The fragmentary remains of baseplates, *c*.0.24m wide, for the E, W and S walls were represented by decayed woodstain. Evidence of the N wall was destroyed during the construction of a succeeding Building PDN4. Short

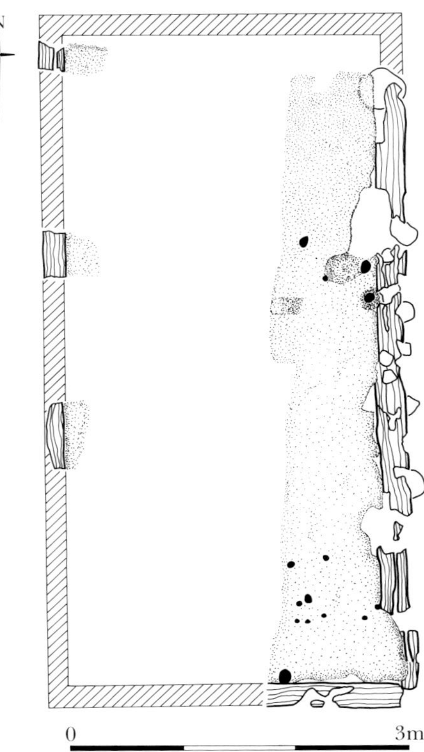

25. Plan of Building PDN3, showing traces of a timber baseplate overlying the padstones of the east wall. Conjectured walls are shown hatched and the internal floor stippled.

lengths of the baseplates for the E and W walls remained *in situ* in the NW and SE corners. These were preserved as parallel timber impressions separated by a narrow band of silt providing evidence that the upper face of the baseplates were cut by a central groove. The abandonment *in situ* of these timbers would suggest that the baseplates were composed of several lengths of timber.

The W, and the greater part of the E, baseplate were supported on rows of levelled, reused Roman tiles, ragstones and unfinished quernstones. These were set within narrow slots dug into the compact levelled silt platform laid over the the remains of the sunken-floored Building PDN2. Beyond the S edge of the infilled sunken area the line of padstones on which the E baseplate was supported gave way to small timbers aligned E-W. In contrast, the baseplates supporting the SE corner and the S wall were laid direct to earth.

Entrance: the similar level of the contemporary internal and external surfaces at the S end of the building suggests, in the absence of more con-

clusive evidence, that the entrance was on the S wall.

Internal features: an unworn, orange-tan, mixed brickearth sand and pebble floor, *c*.0.45m thick, was laid on the compacted silt platform, described above. Five small stakeholes set in this floor, *c*.0.5m from the S wall, probably mark the outer edge of a timber-revetted bench. To the N another group of small stakeholes represent supports for interior furnishings. Evidence of more substantial fixtures in the N part of the building is provided

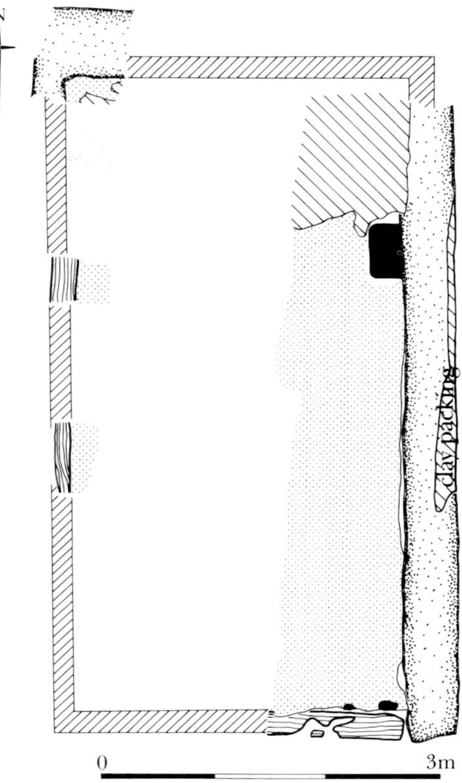

26. Opposite: Part of surface-laid Building PDN3, *looking south-west. The 5 × 100mm scales rest on the internal floor, with the remains of the timber baseplate for the east wall resting on reused quern stones.*

27. Right: Plan showing substantial modifications to Building PDN3, *in which the west wall is retained, but the east and north walls are replaced during construction of Building* PDN4. *The new brickearth surface is shown hatched and the posthole for the temporary roof support in black. Note that the new east and north walls are founded on a mortar bed (cf Figs 25, 30, 33).*

28. Below: Surface-laid Building PDN4, *looking south. The 5 × 100mm scale rests on the internal chalk floor lapping up against the robbed-out baseplate. Note the remains of the burnt partition in the foreground.*

by three larger stakes and a depression marking the position of a free-standing post.

The interior of the building was sealed by a thin silt layer extending across the E wall-line but respecting the S and W wall-lines, implying the demolition of the E but not of the S and W walls. This layer was cut by two stakeholes marking the position of internal supports for the S wall.

Second phase

(Fig 26)

This phase seems to represent temporary occupation of part of the building while substantial modifications were made to the superstructure (Building PDN3-4).

Plan: the N and W wall-lines of the earlier phase were reused but the E wall-line was realigned immediately to the E of the previous wall-line.

Walls: the W wall of the earlier phase was retained.

The N and E walls were supported on rubble- and gravel-filled trenches, capped with yellow mortar (Fig 27).

No structural evidence for a S wall survived but the straight S edge of accumulated resurfacings retained the impression of a timber, which presumably supported a wooden framework acting as a screen or wall.

Internal features: Three successive mortar sand and brickearth floors were found, but were confined to the N end of the building. A very large posthole at the SE corner of these floors, aligned with their S edge, probably marks the position of a roof post set beside the E wall.

The W wall was extended at least 1.5m to the S. The posts inside the S wall of the earlier phase were removed and the wall itself dismantled.

Demolition: the presumed roof post against the E wall was robbed out and the timber retaining the floor surfaces in tne N removed.

Dating: CP3. Laid out over sunken-floored Building PDN2 (CP3); sealed by Building PDN4 (CP4).

Archive ref: PDN81, Group A8.

Building PDN4

(Figs 9a, 10a, 30-31)

First phase

(Figs 30, 31a)

Plan: rectangular surface-laid building, *c*.7.6m N-S × 3.4m E-W, reusing the N, E and W wall-lines of PDN3. The S wall-line was not preserved but lay at least 1.5m to the S of that of PDN3. Its position is estimated on the assumption that the porch constructed in the second phase of this building was built at the mid-point on the W wall.

Walls: probably wooden walls supported on timber baseplates. The N, E and W walls of the second phase of PDN3 were retained.

Internal features: mortar floor overlain by charcoal and burnt wood representing the fragmentary carbonised remains of a wooden bench set against S part of the E wall.

Entrance: probably on the S wall since the internal surface at the N end of the building was 0.5m below the contemporary external surface due to the deliberate raising of the external surface on its E and probably also on its N side.

29. Section across the foundation of the east wall of Building PDN4. Heavy stipple denotes a layer of redeposited charcoal, sealing the padstone and decayed timber plank (PDN3) shown in black.

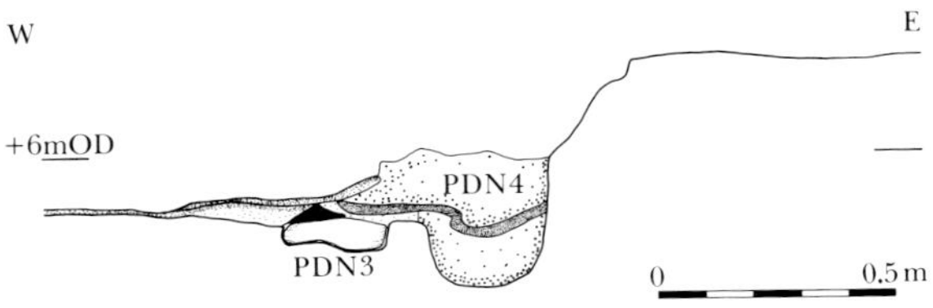

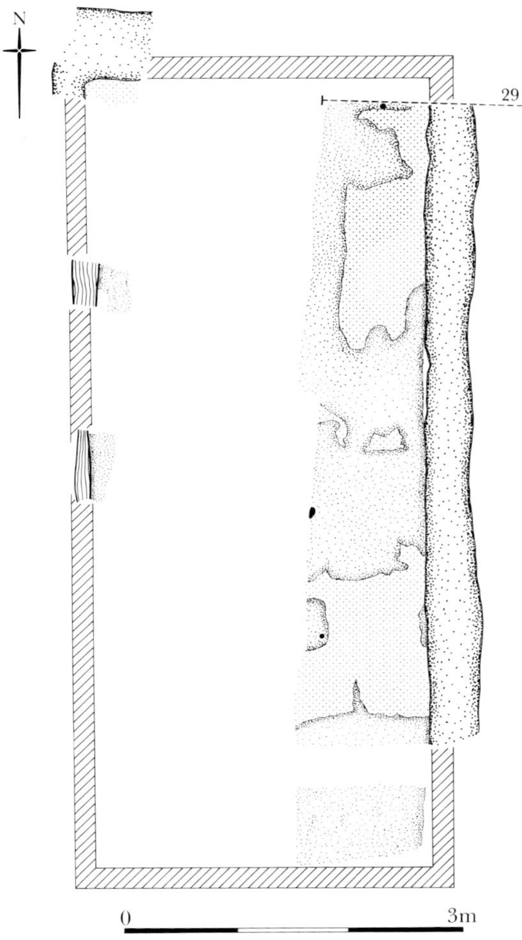

30. Plan of Building PDN4, *showing also the position of the section shown in Fig 29. Light irregular stipple indicates the internal floor, with regular stipple marking the worn areas (cf Figs 27, 32, 33).*

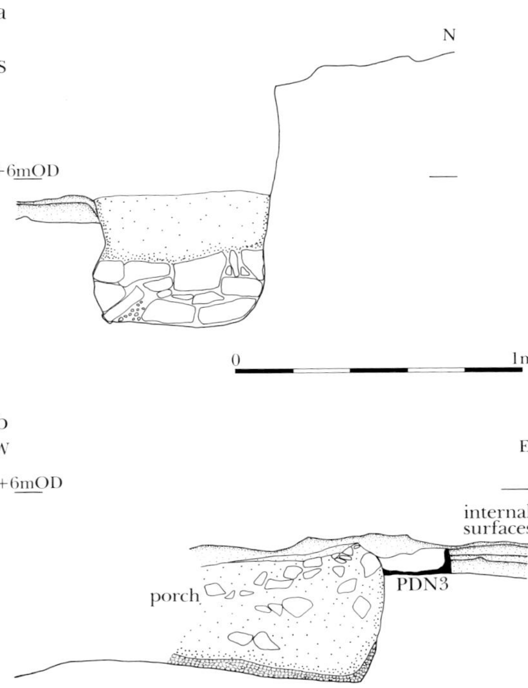

31. a) Section across the north wall foundation of Building PDN4. *b) Section across the porch on the western wall of Building* PDN4. *Note the remains of a timber baseplate for the dismantled section of the west wall, sealed beneath the accumulated porch surfaces.*

Second phase

(Figs 31b, 32-33)

Walls: at least 1.3m of the W wall, but excluding the baseplate, was removed to allow the construction of a doorway and porch.

Entrance: porch with substantial mortary rubble foundations, extending *c.*0.8m beyond the W wall-line. No structural evidence for the porch survived but the preservation of successive brickearth and crushed chalk surfaces indicate that it was roofed.

Internal features: four phases of resurfacing were recorded, including at least three superimposed floors of brickearth and chalk with interleaved occupation debris. The earliest, brickearth, floor was bisected by a narrow slot 0.1m wide, marking the line of an E-W partition *c.*1m S of the N wall, and subdividing the building into two rooms. The line of this partition exactly reflected the limit of the N part of the building temporarily occupied during the construction of the S wall. Two post-holes in the N room represent evidence of internal fixtures rather than structural supports. The brickearth floor in this N room was not resurfaced when a chalk floor was laid in the S room.

The surfaces in both rooms were sealed by the carbonised remains of a wattle hurdle originally forming the partition. It was overlain by a mixed silt/brickearth/mortar layer which raised the internal surface of the building by *c.*0.15m. This surface was cut by a shallow slot on the same alignment as the earlier E-W partition indicating the re-division of the building into two rooms. This slot was infilled before a brickearth floor was laid ending the sub-division of the building.

The N and W walls were dismantled after the construction of the foundation for the NW corner

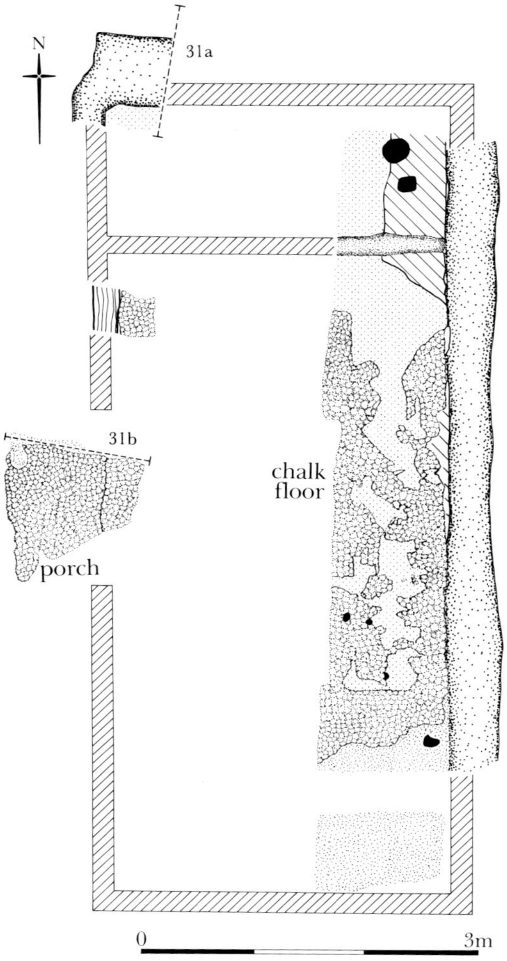

32. Plan of Building PDN4 *after the introduction of a porch to the west and a partition to the north (cf Figs 26, 30, 33); also shown is the position of the sections in Figs 31 (a) and (b).*

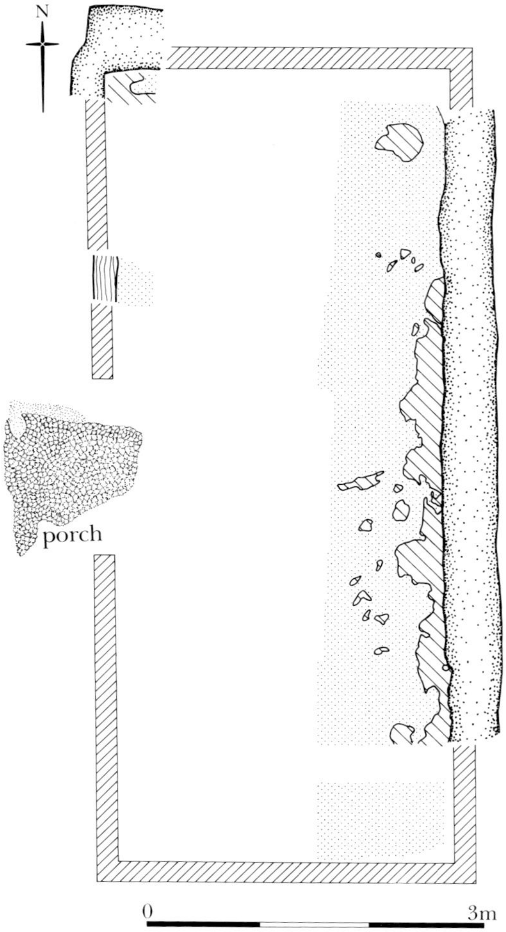

33. Plan of Building PDN4 *after the removal of the partition. The worn brickearth floor is shown hatched (cf Figs 30, 32).*

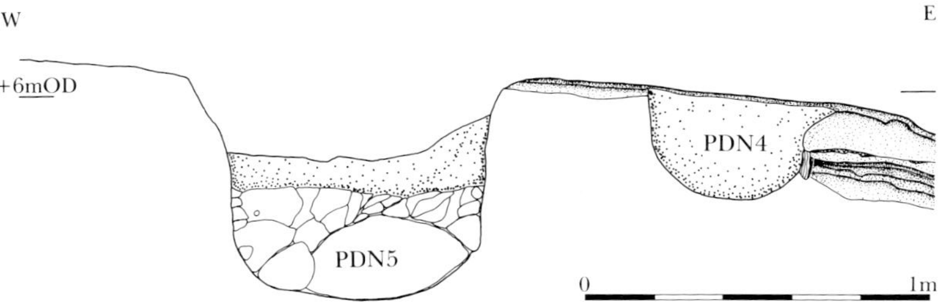

34. Section across the foundation trenches of the west wall and internal surfaces of Buildings PDN4 *and* PDN5.

and W wall of the succeeding Building PDN5.

Dating: CP4. Built around the partially dismantled shell of Building PDN3 (CP3); sealed by Building PDN5 (PDN4).

Archive ref: PDN81, Group A9.

Building PDN5

(Figs 4, 10b, 34-36)

Plan: rectangular surface-laid building *c*.10.1m N-S × *c*.5.0m E-W with a N extension and a porch on the W wall.

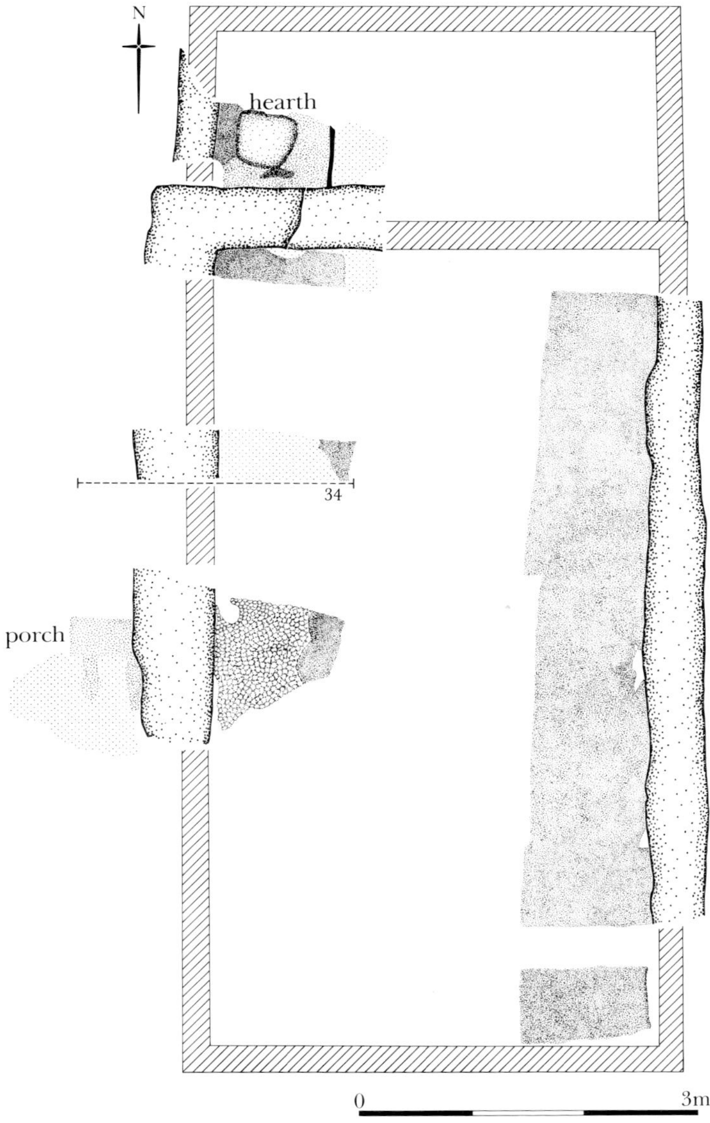

35. Plan showing the construction levels of Building PDN5, and the position of the section shown in Fig 34. Charcoal spread is marked by heavy stipple. Note the modifications to the north-west corner of Building PDN4, the new west wall line and northern extension (cf Fig 33).

Walls: probably wooden walls carried on timber baseplates. The E, and probably also the S, wall of earlier Building PDN4 were retained (Fig 30).

The NW corner and the W wall were supported on mortar beds laid over trenches packed with ragstone and chalk rubble. The N wall foundation was added to the foundation of the earlier Building PDN4 and the W wall foundation was aligned

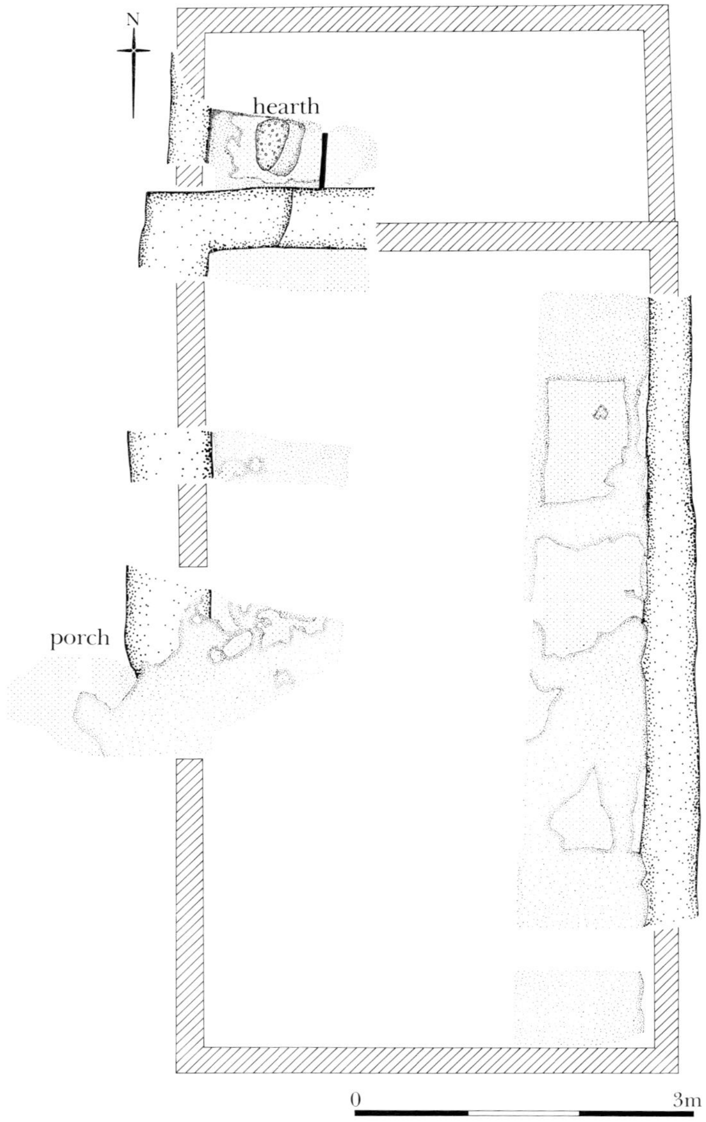

just W of but parallel to, the W wall-line of PDN4, enclosing previously external surfaces.

An extension was added to the N wall. Its W wall was supported on a slot packed with crushed mortar which had previously supported the E wall of Building PDN7.

Entrance: internal surfaces extending over the W wall line indicate the position of a doorway and porch on the same alignment as its predecessor, Building PDN4. No structural evidence for the porch survived but the preservation of successive sand and mortar floors indicate that it was roofed.

36. Plan of Building PDN5, with a gravel-filled hearth-base in the northern extension. The internal surface is shown with light stipple; worn areas with regular stipple.

Internal features: successive silt and sand layers raised the surface inside the W wall-line. These were overlain by a layer of charcoal, up to 35mm thick, spread throughout the building and into the N extension. It had not burnt *in situ* and apparently acted as a final layer of makeup before the introduction of a gravelly sand floor. Sandwiched between the charcoal layer and the floor was a

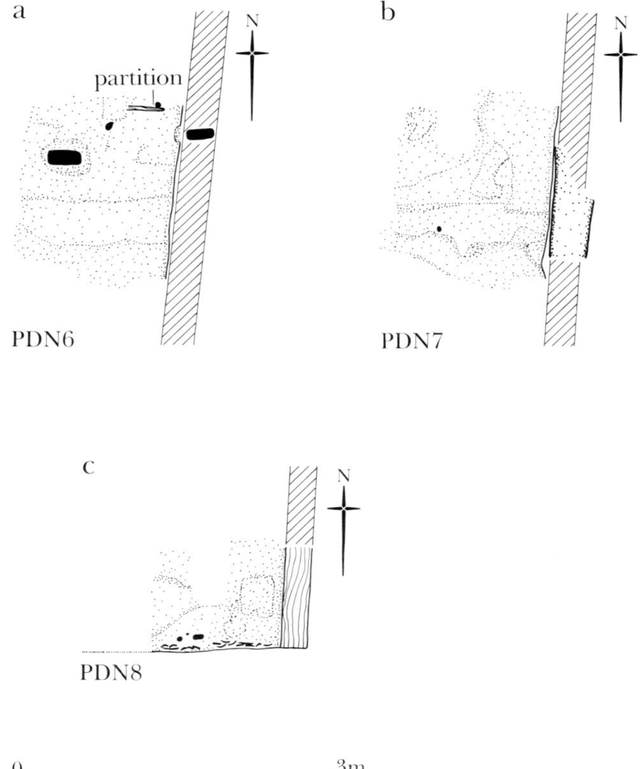

thin layer of silt. This sand floor was sealed by the patchy remains of a later mortar floor.

In the N extension, a similar sand surface abutted a sunken basin 0.52m × 0.48m × 0.26m deep, interpreted as an oven or hearth. Large tile fragments set as hardcore in its base represent the remains of a similar earlier structure. The impression of a plank set on edge in the floor marked the line of a N-S partition, indicating that the extension was subdivided into at least two bays. The sand surface in the extension was sealed by tread with numerous fragments of copper or bronze slag.

The building was carefully dismantled and the timber removed. Its interior was overlain by a sequence of compacted clay /silt dumps forming a carefully prepared external surface over the site. Preserved within these deposits were the corroded ironwork and very decayed remains of the door (see p.88 and Figs 84, 85, 86).

Although the timber had been robbed out, the accumulated floor surfaces along the E wall and the packing within its construction trench preserved the shape and dimensions of dressed timber

37. a) Plan of Building PDN6. *Posts are shown black; and the sequence of very worn brickearth surfaces shown stippled. b) Plan of Building* PDN7. *Note the east wall foundation, later reused for the west wall of the northern extension to Building* PDN5 *(cf Fig 9). Worn internal floors are shown stippled. c) Plan of Building* PDN8, *with carbonised wattles on the line of the south wall (cf Fig 10).*

baseplates, *c.*0.24m sq, on which the superstructure had been supported.

Dating: CP4. Built around the partially dismantled shell of Building PDN4 (CP4); demolished after a coin of 1062 was deposited; sealed by successive external surfaces in use with Buildings PDN8 and PDN9 (CP4 and 5).

Archive ref: PDN81, Group A10.

Building PDN6

(Figs 9a, 37a)

Plan: fragment of surface-laid building, 1.76m × 1.4m.

Walls: probably earthfast posts set at regular intervals. Approx. 1.6m of the E wall-line survived, preserving the impression of one earthfast wooden post, 0.36m E-W × 0.16m N-S. The west face of this post was champfered at the base.

Internal features: *c*.0.80m from the E wall-line the impression of a freestanding earthfast wooden post, 0.30m E-W by 0.14m N-S, marked the position of a probable roof support. A series of at least four very worn beaten earth surfaces had accumulated around this post. The penultimate floor contained the impressions of a short stretch of wattling and of an adjacent small circular stake, marking the line of a shortlived internal partition.

Demolition: E wall dismantled and the upper part of the post removed.

Dating: CP3. Overlies an external surface sealing dark earth dumps to the N of Building PDN2 (CP3); sealed by Building PDN7 (CP3).

Archive ref: PDN81, Group A4.

Building PDN7

(Fig 9b, 37b)

Plan: fragment of surface-laid building, 1.76m × 1.4m E-W. Reuses the E wall-line of Building PDN6.

Walls: probably wooden walls carried on timber baseplates. 1.04m length of the E wall footing survived as shallow slot packed with levelled crushed mortar. The mortar was laid within a wooden form, subsequently removed.

Internal features: a series of at least three superimposed beaten earth floors, the latest with a mortar resurfacing.

Demolition: E wall dismantled and its components removed.

Dating: CP3. Laid out over Building PDN6 (CP3); sealed by Building PDN8 (CP4).

Archive ref: PDN81, Group A4

Building PDN8

(Fig 10b, 11a, 37c)

Plan: a fragment of the SE corner of a surface-laid building, 1.4m E-W × 1.0m N-S.

Walls: a 1.12m length of the S wall-line preserved as single row of burnt wattles. Two stakeholes mark the position of uprights. The recovery of numerous fragments of burnt daub with well-preserved wattle impressions may indicate that the wattle wall was coated in daub.

A 0.92m length of the E wall-line survived as the impression of a horizontally laid plank or sill-beam, *c*.0.24m wide. A thin band of charcoal against its inner edge may be the burnt remains of either wattling or a plank laid on edge against the face of the wall. The use of wattle and daub for the S wall could imply that the timber baseplate described above supported a similar superstructure.

Internal features: one worn mortar floor with brick-earth and silt patching. It was sealed by ashy layers, up to 0.1m thick, extending across the S and E wall-lines indicating that Building PDN8 was destroyed by fire.

Dating: CP4. Overlies Building PDN7 (CP3); contemporary with the occupation and demolition of Building PDN5 (CP4) to the SE; sealed by Building PDN9 (CP5).

Archive ref: PDN81, Group A4.

Building PDN9

(Fig 11b)

Plan: a 1.3m length of the S wall-line of a surface-laid building.

Walls: a 1.3m length of the S wall-line survived as the carbonised remains of a sill beam or plank set within a slot, 0.5m wide. The recovery of numerous daub fragments with well-preserved wattle impressions could imply the use of a wattle and daub wall founded in the sill-beam. It was destroyed by fire.

A substantial stakehole immediately outside the S wall may represent evidence of additional external support for this wall, or alternatively, of independent external supports for the roof.

Internal features: no evidence.

Dating: CP5. Laid out on levelling dumps sealing the fire debris of Building PDN8 (CP4); sealed by Building PDN10 (CP6).

Archive ref: PDN81, Group A11.

Building PDN10

(Fig 11c)

This is the only masonry building described in this report: other similar buildings found in the Cheapside Study Area are discussed elsewhere (Schofield and Allen forthcoming).

Plan: fragment of rectangular surface-laid masonry building, 14m E-W × 5m N-S aligned E-W.

Walls: a 4.6m length of the N wall footing, together with three non-contiguous sections of the S wall footing survived as trenches, between 1.2m - 1.6m wide, filled with roughly coursed chalk and ragstone rubble bonded in gravelly mortar. The S wall trenches were up to 0.80m deep but the N wall trench was over 3m deep. The internal floor sequence overlapped the S wall footing by *c.*0.1m, indicating that the superstructure of the wall itself was less than 1.1m wide. The size, depth and composition of these foundations imply the use of a masonry superstructure. Unfortunately, all traces of the superstructure had been removed in antiquity.

Internal features: three successive gravelly sand, brickearth and mortar floors with patchy brickearth and silt repairs, inter-leaved with thin occupation silts. A contemporary mortar plinth, a rubble post pad, a slot containing three small stakeholes and a carbonised timber with another stakehole represent evidence for internal furnishings rather than freestanding structural supports. The removal of the superstructure suggests the entire building was demolished, not destroyed by fire or allowed to decay.

Dating: CP6, mid to late 12th century. Overlies Building PDN9 (CP5) and associated external surfaces to the S; truncated by brick cellars containing debris deposited in the aftermath of the Great Fire of 1666.

Archive ref: PDN81, Group A12.

Building PDN11

(Figs 4, 10, 38)

Plan: sunken-floored building at least 4.8m N-S × *c.*6m E-W, cut at least 0.7m into the underlying Roman levels.

Walls: a 1.46m length of N wall and a 1.6m length of E wall survived as slots into which post holes up to 300mm in diameter had been cut. There was evidence that planks forming the wall cladding had been slotted into those posts. The timber only survived as stains, and most of the wooden members had been robbed out before the feature was backfilled.

Internal features: mid-tan coloured sand and pebble surface probably served as a working surface during the construction of the building. It was overlain by a tread layer over which was a sand and clay layer acting as a makeup layer for two successive phases of gravel surfacing.

An internal structural feature, marked by a slot 0.2m wide was then introduced, but was only recorded for less than 1m E-W. Lying on the patched brickearth floor which ran up to this slot were fragments of a large storage jar. These features were sealed by a brickearth surface containing many fragments of decayed wood and wattle impressions. The interface between the two surfaces was marked by the clear impressions of grass or rushes.

A number of postholes or post impressions cut into this level probably mark the line of an internal feature rather than a major structural element. The NW corner of a shallow rectangular feature was recorded to the S of this post line. The sunken-floored building was infilled with material including much Roman building debris.

Dating: CP3. Cut through earlier pits (CP2); sealed by later pits (CP4-5).

Archive ref: PDN81, Group B27.

Fish Street Hill (FMO85)

Building FMO1

(Figs 4, 39)

Plan: NW corner of sunken-floored building, at least 3.5m N-S × at least 2.5m E-W, and at least 0.4m deep.

Walls: the N wall-line was represented by a ledge *c.*0.4m wide, standing 0.2m above the base of the sunken area (see below). It was penetrated by at least three postholes, *c.*0.5m deep packed with

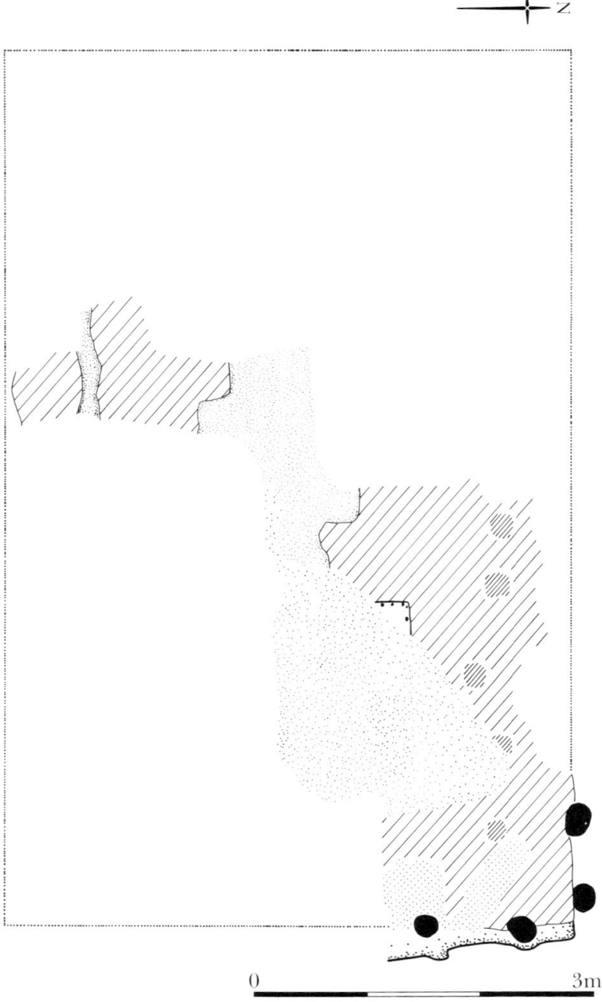

38. Plan of sunken-floored Building PDN11. *The internal brick-earth floor is shown hatched and the conjectured wall dotted. Note the line of post-impressions indicating the position of an internal feature on the north side of the building, with a slot indicating the position of an internal feature on the south side.*

ragstones marking the position of irregularly-spaced square, D-shaped and circular wall posts, respectively *c.*0.15m sq., *c.*0.1m × 0.25m and 0.20m in diameter. The circular upright stood at the intersection of the N and W walls and presumably acted as a corner post. These post impressions were respected by a hard compacted gravel layer spread over the ledge, sealing the ragstone post packing. It may have provided a free-draining bed for the wall cladding. A narrow linear space between the gravel and the side of the sunken area may preserve the impression of planks laid horizontally on edge, originally attached to the uprights.

Decayed wood fragments with the grain aligned N-S represent traces of the timber baseplate supporting the W wall, later robbed out. It was set within a slot, 0.3m wide.

Internal features: a series of thin silt trample layers and compacted sand silt and gravel deposits.

Dating: CP1. Dug into truncated Roman levels; sealed by Building FMO2 (CP2).

Archive ref: FMO85, Group 12.

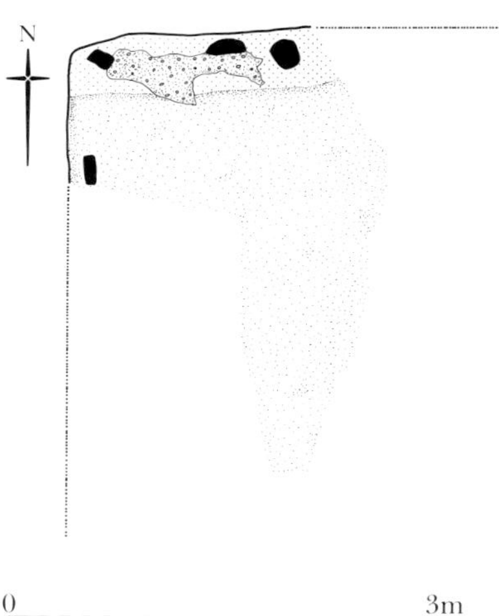

39. Plan of cellared Building FMO2, *the direct replacement of Building* FMO1. *Postholes are shown in black, regular stipple indicates a raised ledge on the north wall; the internal surface is shown with irregular stipple (cf Fig 4).*

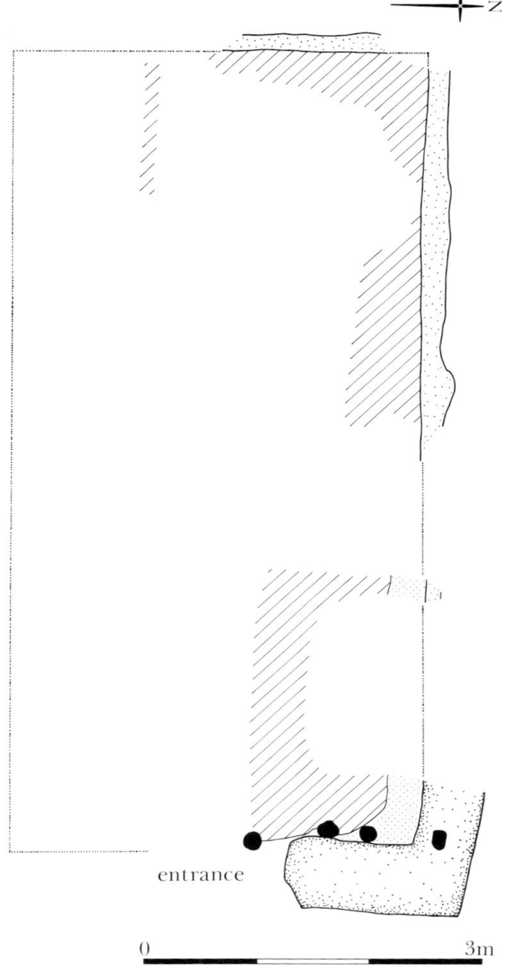

40. Plan of cellared Building FMO3. *Irregular stipple indicates the mortar facing on the north and west walls; the internal brick-earth surface is hatched; postholes are shown in black (cf Fig 4).*

Building FMO2

(Fig 39)

Plan: NW corner of a sunken-floored building, at least 3.5m N-S × at least 2.5m E-W, at least 0.40m deep, reusing the wall-lines of Building FMO1.

Walls: the N wall of Building FMO1 was retained (see above).

A rectangular post impression, 0.20m × 0.08m in a ragstone packed posthole marked the position of at least one earthfast timber upright on the W wall.

Internal features: a series of thin silt trample layers and compacted sand silt and gravel deposits.

Dating: CP2. Overlies Building FMO1 (CP1); cut by Building FMO3 (CP3).

Archive ref: FMO85, Group 12.

Building FMO3

(Figs 4, 40)

Plan: fragment of a sunken-floored building, 8m E-W × at least 3.5m N-S, at least 0.50m deep.

Walls: the W and most of the N wall may have been supported by a stone lining which retained the sides of the sunken area. The NE corner was formed by a right-angled trench, *c*.0.50m wide and 50mm deep, perhaps dug to remove a further length of the stone lining. However, the size and shape of the trench could imply the use of a timber baseplate, later robbed out. The impression of a 0.10m deep post in the base of this trench may represent evidence that at least one timber upright was incorporated into the footing.

Entrance: a gap in the E wall-line 1m from the NE corner may represent evidence of a doorway. At its N side, a 20mm deep posthole may mark the position of an upright forming the N side of the frame.

Internal features: the W and most of the N sides of the sunken area had a stone facing, 0.2m thick and surviving three courses high, composed of irregular mortared courses of dressed ragstone with occasional reused Roman tile fragments. This stone lining was rendered on its internal face. Inside, and parallel to, the NE corner was a row of post impressions, *c*.0.1m deep, which, together with a linear slot 0.2m wide and 0.15m deep, may represent structural supports or internal fixtures placed against the walls.

Accumulated brickearth and beaten earth floors represented the internal floor sequence. These were overlain by a layer of masonry rubble sealing the E wall-line and the E section of the N wall-line raising the internal surface by *c*.0.3m.

Dating: CP3. Dug through Building FMO2 (CP2); sealed by Building FMO4 (CP4).

Archive ref: FMO85, Group 13.

Building FMO4

(not illustrated)

Plan: a fragment of sunken-floored building, at least 9m E-W × at least 3.5m N-S and at least 0.5m deep, reusing the N and W wall-lines of Building FMO3.

Walls: the W wall and part of the N wall of Building FMO3 were retained. The N wall-line was extended at least 1m to the E. East of the masonry facing, it was represented by a slot, cutting the masonry rubble spread, sealing Building FMO3. Only *c*.0.4m of this feature was observed but it may mark the position of a timber baseplate, later removed.

Internal features: silt re-surfacings.

Dating: CP4. Replaced Building FMO3 (CP3); cut by pit (CP5).

Archive ref: FMO85, Group 13.

Milk Street (MLK76)

Building MLK1

(Figs 14, 41-4, 89)

Plan: a fragment of a sunken-floored building, at least 3m E-W × at least 4.2m N-S and at least 1.5m deep, with an entrance on the E wall. The position of the N and W walls are estimated on the basis that the upward slope of the internal floors indicates the position of the W and N wall-lines immediately outside the limit of excavation. Four phases in the development of this structure have been identified, and are described below, while the reconstruction plan shown in Fig 44 combines evidence from phases 1-3.

First Phase

(Fig 41)

Walls: the S wall was represented by at least two tiers of decayed planks, laid horizontally on edge. Three post impressions, *c*.0.2m in diameter, along

41. Plan of sunken-floored Building MLK1, *first phase. Post impressions are shown in black; the internal surface with light stipple (cf Figs 14, 42-44).*

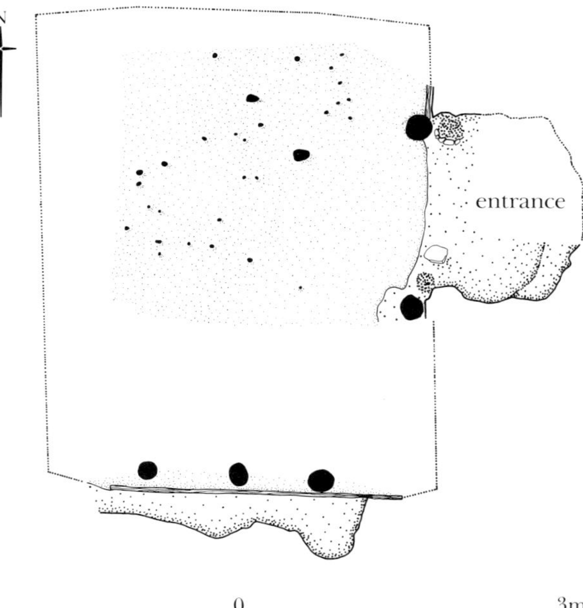

the wall-line mark the position of uprights supporting the S wall. The middle post, in contrast to those set to either side, had been deeply driven in to a depth of 0.6m. The space between the planking and the side of the sunken area was packed with rubbly silt.

The E wall was represented by the remains of decayed planking, supported by two posts of which only the impressions survived.

Entrance: the entrance, set off-centre on the E wall, extended at least 0.7m beyond the wall-line. Access was by way of a ramp to ground level. The threshold of the doorway was below that of the internal surface. A threshold bar was provided by the lowest tier of the planking forming the E wall.

A post impression on the N side of the entrance, together with a ragstone post pad and a depression on the S side, mark the position of uprights forming the door frame. The absence of evidence for uprights at the outer surviving corner of the entrance implies that it was not a roofed porch.

Internal features: 30 stake holes penetrating the floor represented evidence of internal fittings. A sequence of very worn beaten-earth surfaces had accumulated around the entrance.

Second phase

(Figs 42, 44b)

Walls: a brickearth post pad in the N may represent a repair to the presumed NE corner of the building.

Entrance: the doorframe was dismantled and the ramp's surface lowered. A collapsed plank lying across the entrance represented the remains of an upright board at the threshold. A ragstone pad was laid to the S of the earlier pad and a shallow depression was recorded at the N side of the doorway. A narrow slot with the decayed remains of a plank set horizontally on edge and packed with ragstone and tile fragments represents a replacement of the threshold bar. A new ragstone pad in the S suggests that the door post was replaced at the same time.

Third phase

(Fig 43)

Walls: At least two of the posts supporting the S wall were replaced. On the S side of the doorway, a 0.1m length of a slot was recorded, packed with vertical fragments of ragstone and tile. This may

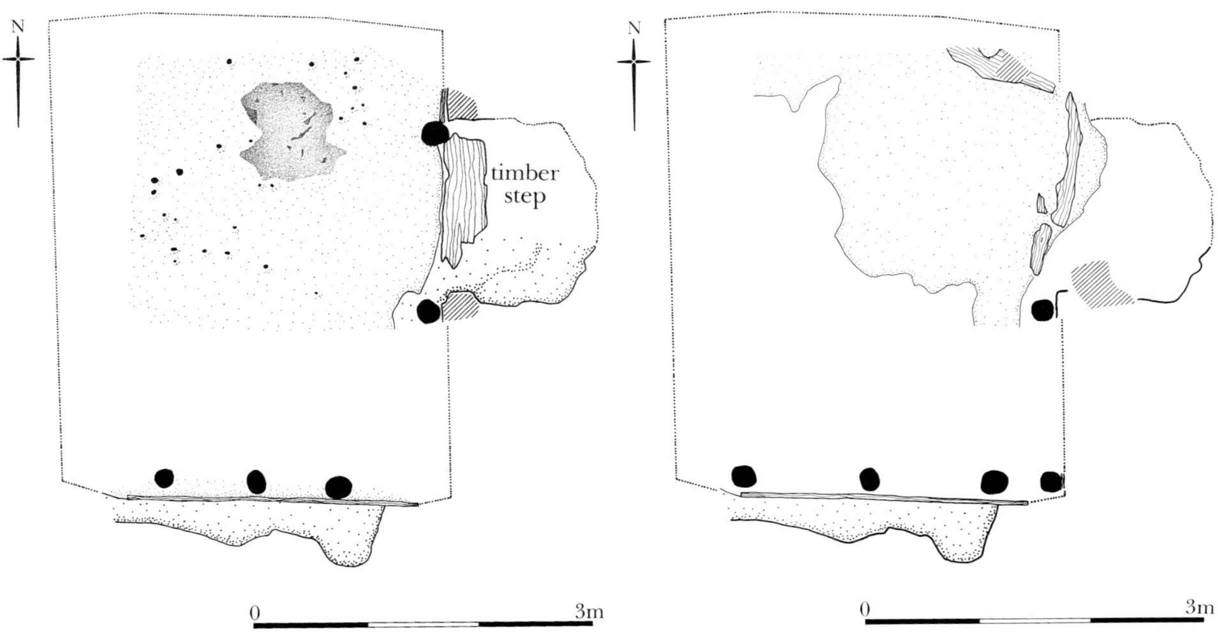

42. Plan of sunken-floored Building MLK I, second phase. The hearth is shown shaded; the brickearth postpads hatched (cf Figs 41, 43, 44).

43. Plan of sunken-floored Building MLK I, third phase, after the rebuilding of the south wall (cf Figs 41, 42, 44).

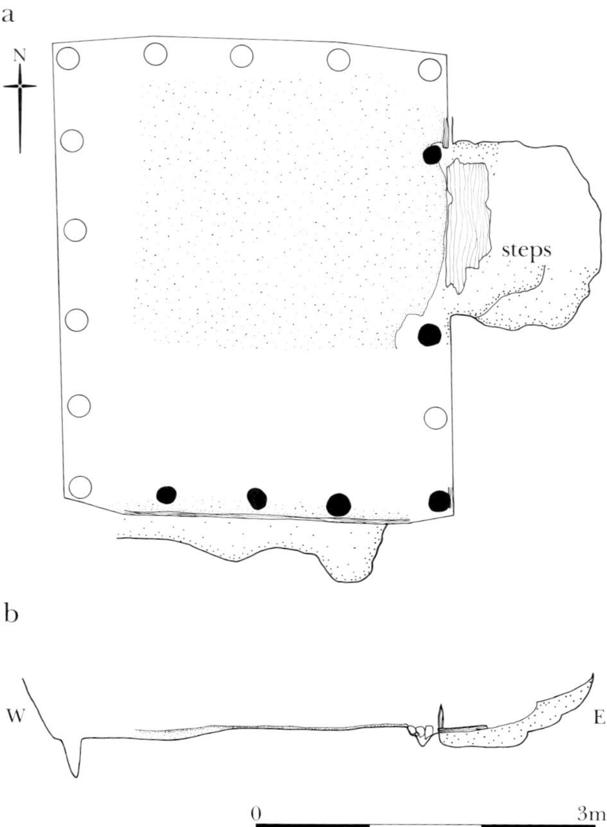

44. a) Alternative reconstruction of the plan of sunken-floored Building MLK I *(by Valerie Horsman & Christine Milne) combining the evidence from phases 1-3. Note the remains of timber plank stairs, and the equidistant spacing of posts. Posts found are shown black; conjectured posts are shown open (cf Figs 41-43). b) Section across sunken-floored Building* MLK I, *with the remains of planked earthern steps shown with light stipple.*

have secured planking set parallel to the S section of the original E wall. It was aligned with the remains of planking in the SE corner, retained by an earthfast post and may represent a modification to, or rebuilding of, the E wall. Two posts on the E wall were replaced.

Internal features: successive beaten-earth floors *c.*0.2m thick with gravel, brickearth and wood chip lenses. Some of these surfaces extended into the entrance, overlapping the threshold. A spread of ash and charcoal with evidence of *in situ* scorching represented evidence of a crude hearth.

Accumulated fragmentary beaten-earth surfaces, 0.5m thick, sealed traces of decayed wood in the NE corner, perhaps representing the remains of a planked floor. This was laid over a compact organic layer.

Fourth phase

Walls: the walls of the earlier phase were retained but a shallow depression in the NW may mark the position of an additional post. The accumulated infill of the sunken area was cut by an oval feature dug down to the level of the latest phase three floor surface.

Internal features: a series of fragmentary beaten-earth surfaces filled the oval feature before the building was finally dismantled and the majority of the wall posts removed.

Dating: CP I. Cut into truncated Roman levels: cut by Building MLK2 (CP2).

Archive ref: MLK76, Period VIIIa-VIIIc.

Building MLK2

(Fig 14)

Plan: a fragment of sunken-floored building, including the NW corner and a length of the S wall. It was at least 2.1m E-W × 3.2m N-S and at least 0.75m deep.

Walls: the N wall-line was marked by a trench filled with gravelly brickearth in which was preserved the impression of a circular post set against the side of the sunken area.

Internal features: a beaten-earth surface 50mm thick.

Dating: CP2. Cut into Building MLK1 (CP1); cut by modern features.

Archive ref: MLK76 Period IX.

Building MLK 3

(not illustrated)

Plan: the N wall of a possible sunken-floored building, 1.9m N-S, unknown E-W; depth 0.35m, recorded in section only.

Walls: impression of a post set outside the edge of the sunken area may represent evidence of its N wall-line or an external roof support.

Internal features: brickearth surface, 0.1m thick, over which were traces of decayed timber planking, sealed by the organic silt dumps which filled the sunken area.

Dating: uncertain. Cut into truncated Roman levels; apparently sealed by horizon of dark grey silts (CP1).

Archive ref: MLK76, Period VIII.

Building MLK4

(Fig 14)

Plan: SE corner of surface-laid building, at least 1.7m E-W × at least 5.5m N-S.

First phase

Walls: a single post, later robbed out, indicated the position of the E wall.

Internal features: silt make-up, capped by a very thin brickearth floor, survived to the E of the wall post impression. It was sealed by layer of silty daub destruction debris, 0.2m thick, compensating for subsidence.

Second phase

Walls: the E wall-line was marked by the impressions of three earthfast posts. One of these posts may have replaced the earlier post. The line of the S wall was marked by a trench in which the impression of at least one circular earthfast post was preserved. It stood at the junction of the S and E walls and presumably acted as a corner post.

Internal features: a brickearth floor 50mm thick was laid up to the E wall. A scatter of stakes cutting the floor represent evidence of internal fittings. These were sealed by a layer of silt and charcoal, marking its disuse. A shallow trench with the impression of a post at its S end lay immediately inside, and parallel to, the S part of the E wall.

Dating: CP2. Laid out over the dark earth horizon (CP1); sealed by Building MLK5 (CP2).

Archive ref: MLK76, Period XIa-XIb.

Building MLK5

(not illustrated)

Plan: a small fragment of a surface-laid building was observed.

Walls: a slot represented the S wall-line.

Internal features: two superimposed brickearth floors, *c*.50mm thick, with interleaving coccupation deposits. The earlier floor was scorched in the S. Two small posts cutting through the floor provide evidence of internal fittings. The floor was overlain in the N by a small area of silty crushed daub. A small fragment of brickearth above it represents the floor of an overlying building or repair.

Dating: CP2. Overlay Building MLK4 (CP2); cut by later pits (CP3-4).

Archive ref: MLK76, Period XIc.

Watling Court (WAT78)

Building WAT1

(Figs 17, 45)

Plan: a fragment of a rectangular sunken-floored building, at least 2.2m E-W × 3.6m N-S, and between 0.4m - 1.2m deep.

Walls: s wall-line represented by slot in which the impressions of upright posts were preserved. At least one post, 0.2m × 0.1m was D-shaped. Decayed woodstain represented the fragmentary remains of a wooden lining retaining the side of the sunken area. The space between the lining and the side of the sunken area was packed with silt.

The N wall-line was represented by circular post impressions *c*.0.2m in diameter, marking the positions of shallowly-set, irregularly spaced uprights.

Internal features: a beaten-earth floor, 0.1m thick, with patches of clay and brickearth was sealed by the clay-silt dumps which infilled the sunken area. In contrast to the s wall, all the timber from the N wall had been removed.

Dating: CP3. Overlay earlier pits (CP1-2); cut by Building WAT2 (CP4).

Archive ref: WAT78, Period xa, Building U.

Building WAT2

(Figs 17, 46)

Plan: SE corner of a rectangular sunken-floored building, *c*.12.7m E-W × at least 5.6m N-S, by at least 0.7m deep. No trace of the w wall survived although its approximate line was established.

Walls: the s wall was represented by the decayed remains of an inner and outer skin of planks supported by at least five posts, *c*.0.2m square, the impressions of which were preserved in clay/silt packing filling the cavity between the planking. These posts were set at regular 1m intervals in a slot, *c*.0.2m wide. The space between the wooden wall and the side of the sunken area was, like the cavity, packed with clay/silt. A rectangular post erected between the wall and the side of the sunken area was part of the original construction, but a small post set against its inner face probably represents a later addition.

The E wall was represented by the decayed remains of single skin of planking. Silt was packed between the planking and the side of the sunken area. No evidence of uprights retaining the planking was recovered.

Internal features: a planked floor butting up against the s and E walls. Successive floors superimposed on it were almost entirely of beaten-earth. The

45. Plan of cellared Building WAT1. *Post impressions are shown in black; packing in the wall trench is shown with regular stipple and the internal floor with irregular stipple (cf Fig 17).*

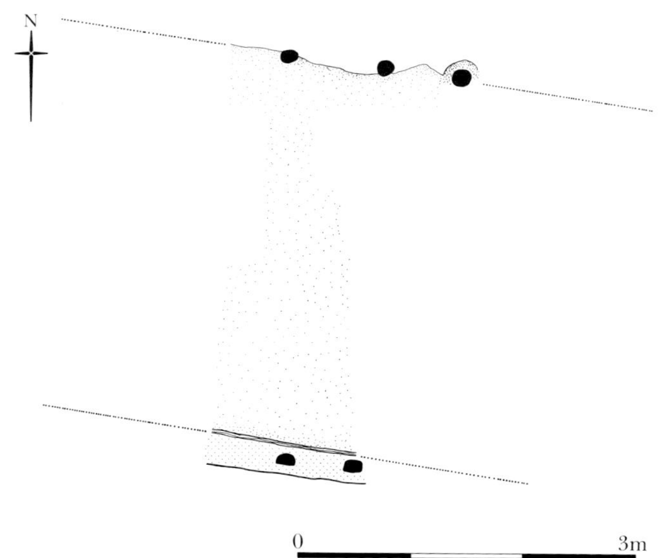

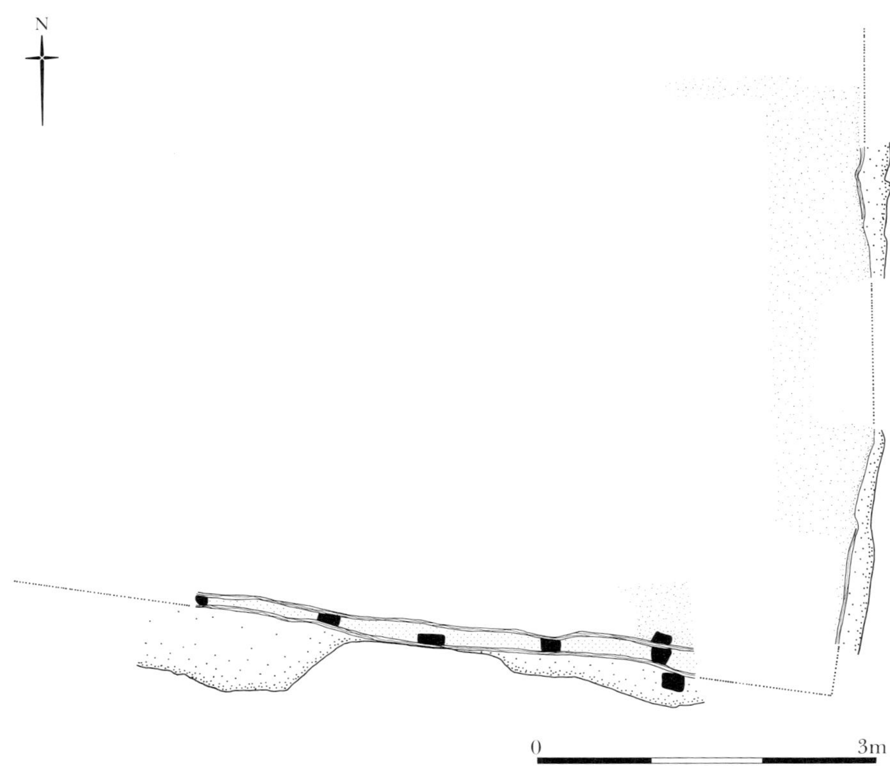

sunken area was backfilled with dumped silt, presumably after the removal of the E wall uprights.

Dating: CP4. Dug through Building WAT1 (CP3); cut by pits (CP4).

Archive ref: WAT78, Period xb, Building v.

46. *Plan of the south-east corner of cellared Building* WAT2. *Note that while the south wall has a double skin of planks, the east wall has a single plank face. The southern 'cavity wall' is indicated with regular stipple and the internal floor with a light stipple (cf Fig 17).*

Building WAT3

(Figs 17, 47-9)

Plan: a fragment of rectangular sunken-floored building, *c*.5.4m E-W × 13.4m N-S and 2.3m deep. The position of the W wall is estimated on the assumption that the surviving W floor joist was laid at the mid-point on the N wall.

First phase

Walls: the E wall was represented by the decayed remains of an inner and outer skin of planks. This plank boarding was supported by at least four posts, *c*.0.2m square, the impressions of which were preserved in the clay/silt packing which filled the cavity. The posts were carried on a timber baseplate set in a slot with silt packing along the inside. The space between the wall and the side of the sunken area was also packed with silt. The wall itself sloped inwards at a slight angle and had obviously sagged.

In contrast the S wall was represented by the remains of a single skin of planking supported by at least four posts preserved as impressions in the silt/clay packing between the cladding and the side of the sunken area. The posts were set at regular 0.9m intervals on the base of the sunken area, three were 0.2m square and one was D-shaped.

The N wall was represented by the decayed remains of a skin of plank boarding rising from the outer edge of a decayed timber baseplate (see Fig 49). It was laid in a slot with silt/clay packing. The space between the wall and the side of the sunken area was packed with silt.

47. Plan of cellared Building WAT3, *first phase. Dense stipple indicates the internal surface in the north; regular stipple marks the silt wall packing (cf Figs 17, 48, 49).*

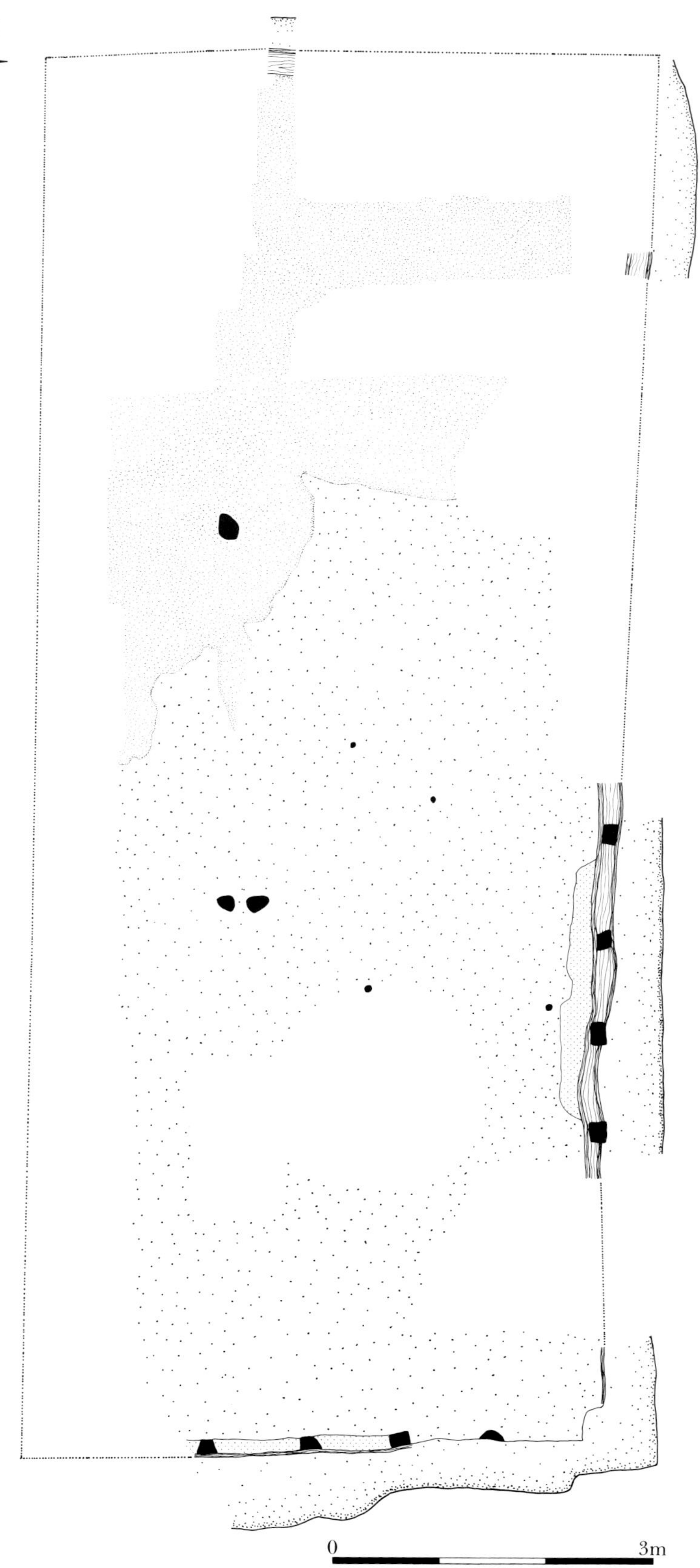

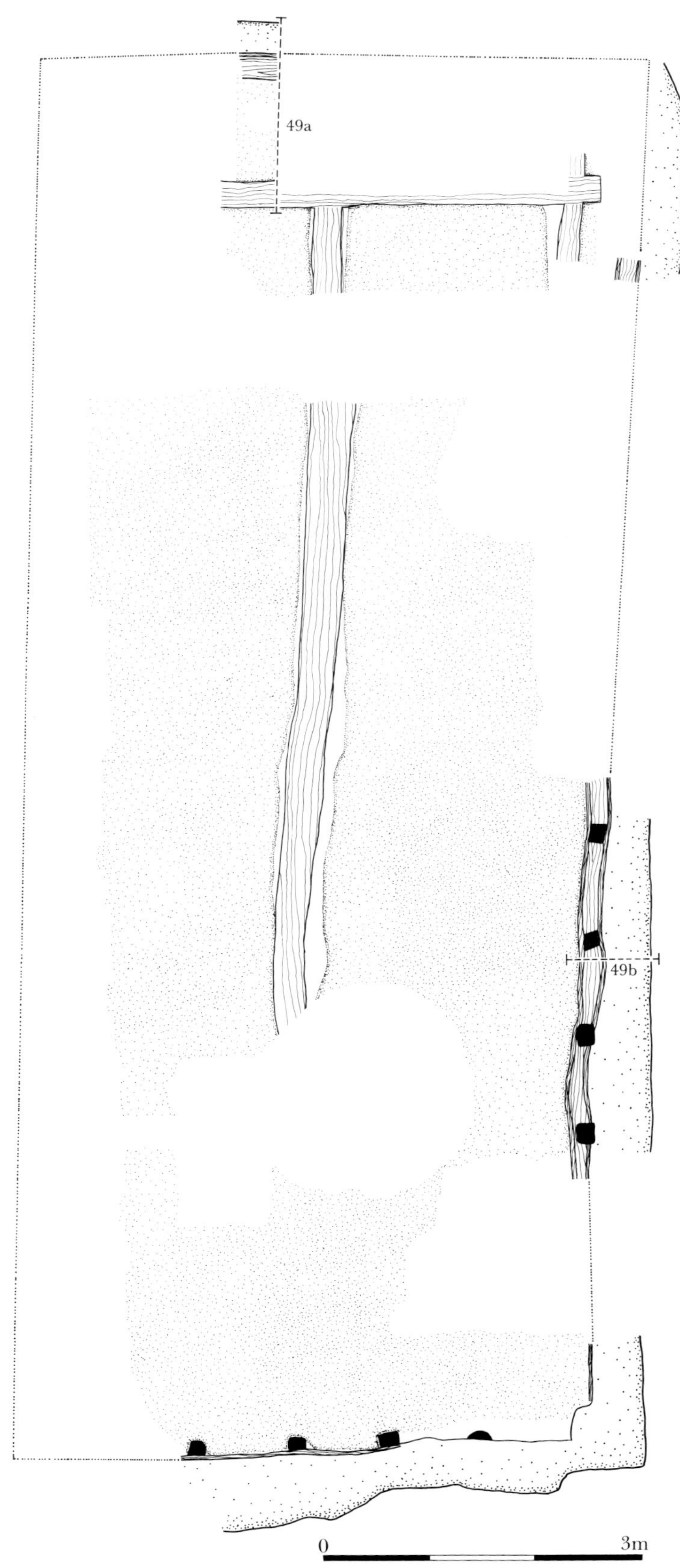

48. Plan of cellared Building WAT3*, second phase, showing the joists for a timber floor (cf Fig 47). For sections across the wall line, see Fig 49a & b.*

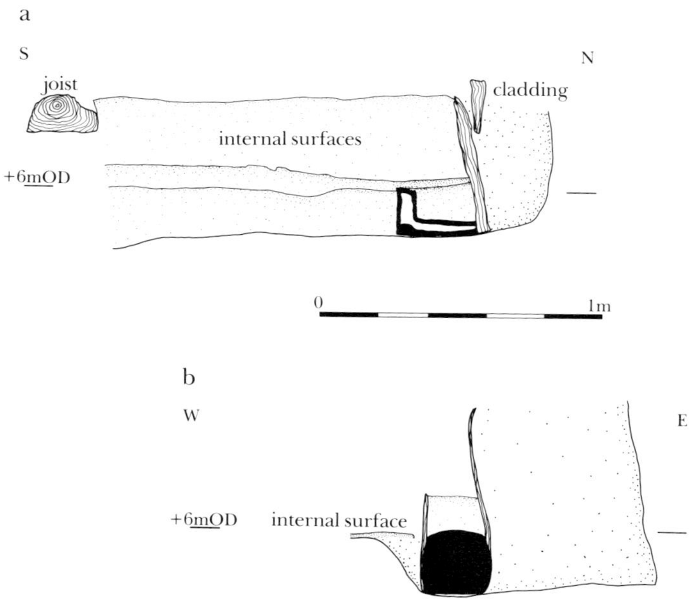

Internal features: compacted brickearth surface laid over a layer of iron slag, 0.2m thick, lapping against the N wall. This surface did not extend into the S part of the building. In the S, thin layers of charcoal and ash representing hearth waste sealed the base of the sunken area. A scatter of stakes may represent evidence of fittings within the cellar, later removed. These were sealed by successive beaten-earth resurfacings. The latest of these surfaces was sealed by a plank floor raised 0.1m above the earlier surface. This had been supported on at least three D-shaped timber beams, up to 0.4m thick, set in shallow slots. The joists aligned N-S were apparently jointed another aligned E-W. One of the N-S beams was laid on a plank.

49. a) Section across part of cellared Building WAT3, *showing the baseplate with a shoulder and the remnants of timber wall cladding. Note the joist from a later phase of flooring. b) Section across the east wall of Building* WAT3. *Note the squared baseplate and remains of a planked wall with infill. For position of sections, see Fig 48.*

Third phase

(not illustrated)

Walls: the S wall was retained. Some 0.15m inside the E wall-line, the decayed remains of planking supported on a timber baseplate were recorded. The impression of an upright post was preserved in silt packing between this planking and the original E wall. A second post, 0.2m to the S of the first, was inserted after an internal surface had been laid.

Internal features: the plank floor was sealed by a silt layer, 0.1m thick, mixed with brickearth and charcoal. It was overlain by the patchy remains of a sandy mortar floor. This floor was sealed by a highly organic layer. In the extreme S, a brickearth floor had similar organic material mixed in with it.

The latest floor surface was cut by an oval pit. This was filled with rubble and capped with creamy mortar, which spread out over the earlier surface to form a rough layer of rubble. A loose ash/charcoal horizon above this represents evidence of a bonfire prior to backfilling.

Dating: CP4. Cut into truncated Roman levels; cut by pits (CP4).

Archive ref: WAT78, Period xb-e, Building W.

Building WAT4

(not illustrated)

Plan: fragment of a sunken-floored building, at least 4.5m E-W × at least 4.9m N-S and at least 0.2m deep.

Walls: no evidence.

Internal features: the impressions of three posts penetrated the base of the feature. These were sealed by the earliest beaten-earth floor indicating a non-structural function. Successive layers of silt mixed with daub and brickearth may represent later superimposed floor surfaces or the backfilling of the sunken area.

Dating: CP3. Cuts earlier pits (CP1-3); cut by post-medieval intrusions.

Archive ref: WAT78, Period X.

Well Court (WEL79)

Building WEL1

(not illustrated)

Plan: a sunken-floored building, recorded in section only, at least 1.1m E-W, unknown N-S, 0.2m-0.7m deep.

Walls: the remains of decayed earthfast post, 0.15m in diameter. driven 0.4m into the base of the sunken area, 0.2m from its E side. Clay/silt packing filled the space between the post and the side of the sunken area.

Internal features: beaten-earth floor 0.1m thick, with patches of brickearth, mortar and ragstone chips. It was sealed by silt dumps filling the sunken area.

Dating: CP1. Dug into truncated Roman strata; cut by 12th-century stone undercroft (CP5).

Archive ref: WEL79, Period VIII.2.

Building WEL2

(not illustrated)

Plan: S side of the entrance to a surface-laid building, at least 2.2m N-S.

Walls: three intercutting postholes mark the position of successive uprights, *c*.0.2m-0.3m in diameter, supporting the S side of the doorframe. At least one of these contained a ragstone pad on which the upright stood. The postholes were set back from a contemporary street to the E.

Internal features: a beaten-earth floor *c*.0.1m thick extended beyond the W wall-line, overlapping the E edge of the street metalling.

Dating: presumably CP1-2. Overlay the second street surface; sealed by Buildings WEL3 and WEL4 (CP2).

Archive ref: WEL79, Period X.2.

Building WEL3

(Figs 19, 50, 91, 92)

Plan: SW corner of a surface-laid building, at least 1.5m E-W × at least 1.6m N-S.

Walls: the line of the W wall was preserved by a double row of postholes marking the position of paired posts, *c*.0.15m × 0.1m, spaced at irregular intervals within a slot. A single line of stakeholes ran between the postholes indicating that the uprights had supported a wattle framework. The slot was packed with silty clay and fragments of

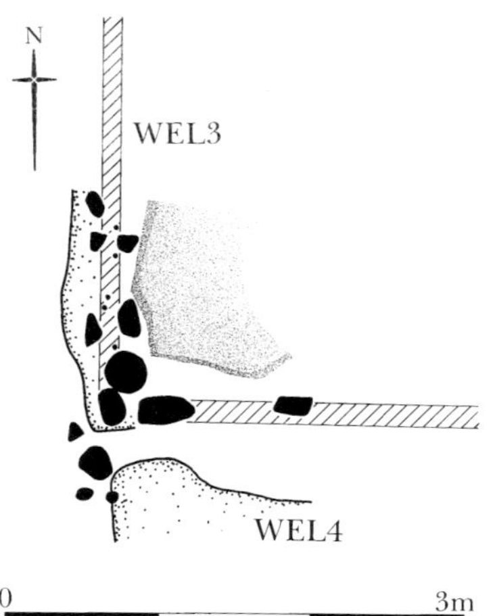

50. Plan of the south-east corner of Building WEL3. *Postholes are shown black; the oven shaded. This Building abutted the pre-Conquest street surface beneath Bow Lane to the west, and the fragmentary remains of Building* WEL4 *to the south.*

ragstone, quern stone and *tegulae* securing the wattles and adjacent posts.

By contrast the line of the S wall was marked by two of a single row of postholes, respectively 0.38m × 0.20m and 0.26m × 0.14m, marking the position of at least two earthfast posts. Two postholes at the junction of the S and W walls mark the position of circular and oval earthfast corner posts, *c.*0.2m in diameter. A third posthole, 0.14m × 0.12m × 0.25m deep, may represent evidence of an additional external earthfast roof support.

Internal features: no floor surfaces survived but an oven, 1m E-W × 1.1m N-S, with slightly curved sides was recorded in the SW corner. Its base was constructed of alternating layers of gravel, re-used Roman tiles, and brickearth. Its walls survived 0.1m above the base. The superstructure was formed of brickearth cladding on a frame of 33 angled stakes. The floor was baked hard but although scorched it was remarkably clean. Carbonised grain was recovered from the oven. The remains of the oven were sealed by a layer of silty daub, 0.1m-0.2m thick including large parts of its superstructure and fragments of quern stone.

The building was dismantled and its timber components removed.

Dating: CP2. Overlay Building WEL2 (CP1-2); sealed by Building WEL5 (CP3). Archaeomagnetic samples from the oven were dated to the second half of the 10th century.

Archive ref: WEL79, Period XI.1-XI.2, Building R.

Building WEL4

(Figs 19, 50)

Plan: NW corner of a sunken floored feature, at least 1.6m E-W × at least 4.2m N-S and 0.4m deep.

Walls: a group of small posts and stakes packed with silty clay mark the position of the NW corner. These were replaced by a large post.

Internal features: the base of the sunken area was sealed by layers of ash and burnt twigs which overlapped its N edge and probably represented rake-off from the oven in the adjacent Building WEL3. Carbonised grain was recovered from this deposit.

Dating: CP2. Overlay Building WEL2. Sealed by destruction debris which also sealed Building WEL3.

Archive ref: WEL79, Period XI.

Building WEL5

(not illustrated)

Walls: all that survived of this surface-laid building was a fragment of the W wall. A row of three postholes set back from the contemporary street, marked the position of earthfast posts supporting the wall, parallel to the W wall of earlier Building WEL3. The southernmost was a setting for two posts 0.2m - 0.25m in diameter, and the northernmost had a tile pad in its base.

Dating: presumably CP3. Overlay Building WEL3 (CP2); sealed by Building WEL6 (CP4).

Archive ref: WEL79, Period XII.1.

Building WEL6

(Figs 20, 51)

Plan: a fragment of a surface-laid building, at least 6.1m N-S × at least 4m E-W.

Walls: the line of the W wall was indicated by the impressions of three posts, *c.*0.11m in diameter, set at regular 0.7m intervals, within a shallow trench at least 0.2m wide. The posts were secured by rubble packing laid within the trench.

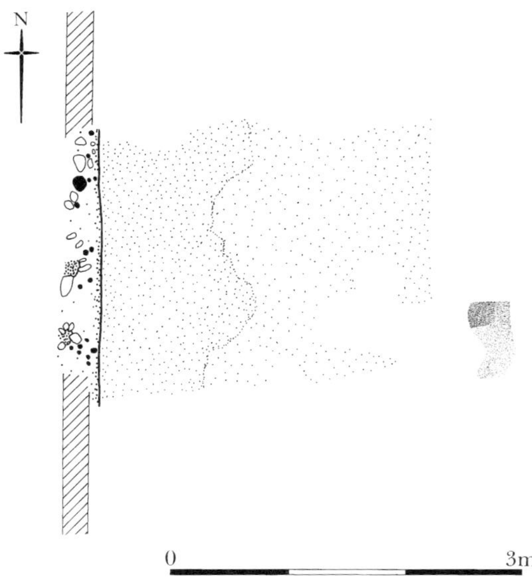

51. Plan of Building WEL6*, which sealed Building* WEL3*, showing the west wall line. Light stipple denotes the internal floor; the hearth is shaded; post impressions and stakeholes are shown in black. The stones in the wall trench probably represent post-settings.*

Immediately inside the line of posts, the decayed remains of wattling marked the position of a screen retaining the walling material. The rubble packing around the post impressions was overlain by clay-silt filling the trench. All the timber posts had been removed.

Internal features: a silty-clay floor 0.1m thick was sealed by accumulated occupation deposits abutting the W wall-line. Further E a series of ash layers sealed by patches of clay and brickearth probably represent waste from a hearth or oven of which a small part survived. Its brickearth base, scorched and baked hard by use, was 0.2m thick and rested 0.3m below contemporary floor level. It was twice re-surfaced and these later surfaces had a slightly raised rim, suggesting that it was lined at least to floor level. The feature was backfilled with burnt and unburnt brickearth fragments, representing collapsed lining.

Dating: CP4. Overlay Building WEL4 (CP2); cut by pits (CP4).

Archive ref: WEL79, Period XII.2, Building S.

Building WEL7

(Fig 52)

Plan: the E wall and entrance porch of a sunken-floored building 4.7-6.5m E-W × at least 1.8m N-S and at least 1m deep. It was mainly recorded in section, but although the W wall-line itself was not preserved, the survival of earlier strata indicates that the length of the building cannot have been greater than 6.5m.

Walls: the sharp profile of the sunken area suggested it was originally plank-lined although no other evidence for this survived. Decayed wood

52. a) Section across sunken-floored Building WEL7*, showing the remains of a baseplate set in a trench. b) Section across the entrance on the east wall of sunken-floored Building* WEL7*, showing the remains of a wall trench (regular stipple) and step to the east.*

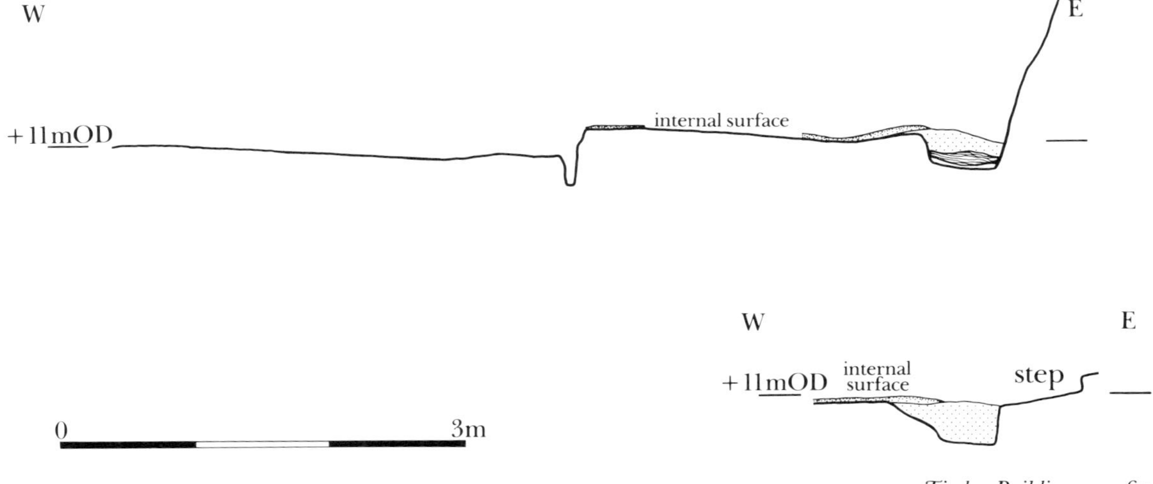

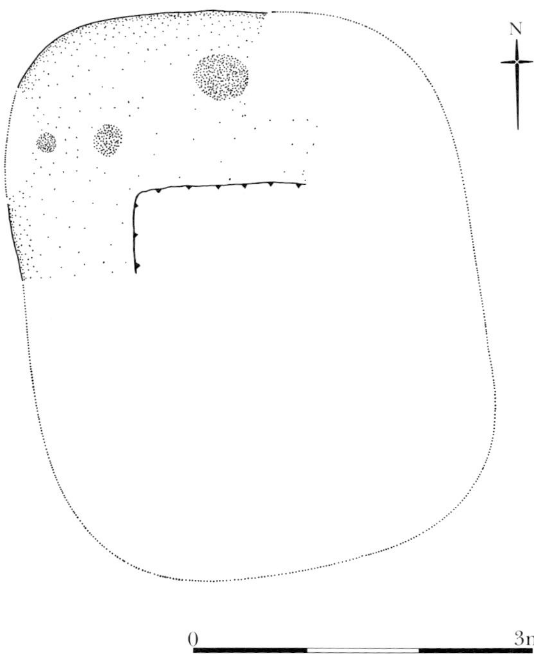

53. Plan of the north-west corner of sunken-floored Structure IRO1, *showing the position of post impressions (heavy stipple), and internal pit. Conjectured walls are shown dotted.*

represented the fragmentary remains of a timber baseplate on which the E wall was supported. It rested on a thin levelled clay-silt bed within a trench. The remains of silty clay packing was preserved above the baseplate.

Entrance: a porch extended beyond the E wall-line, and the N wall-line was marked by a slot. In the NE corner, the fragmentary remains of the lowest step were preserved 0.1m high. A threshold bar was provided by the baseplate of the E wall.

Internal features: a thin brickearth floor in the S gave way to a beaten-earth surface in the N. In the W, a feature at least 1.1m E-W and 0.2m deep, was cut through the base of the sunken area. A stakehole at the base of its E side may have retained a wooden lining. With the exception of the baseplates described above all the timber was removed before the sunken area was infilled with tipped dumps of silt mixed with clay,brickearth and daub.

Dating: CP2-4. Overlay the dark earth horizon (?CP1); cut by pits (CP4).

Archive ref: WEL79, Period XI, Building T.

Ironmonger Lane (IRO80)

Building IRO1

(Figs 21, 53)

Plan: NW corner of oval sunken-floored building, probably 4m E-W × 5m N-S and 1.1m deep.

Walls: the line of the N wall was represented by the impressions of three earthfast posts, marking the positions of two posts in the NW corner and one at the mid-point on the wall. The latter may have acted as a roof support, perhaps carrying the N end of a ridge pole.

Internal features: the base of the sunken area was cut by a rectangular feature at least 1.4m E-W × 1.7m N-S and 0.2m deep. It was filled with green-flecked organic material containing large quantities of animal bone, including antler cores, and charcoal. This feature was sealed by silty gravels, 0.3m thick, slumping in from the sides of the sunken area and partly filling it. These were sealed by a layer of compacted organic debris which acted as a floor surface. It was overlain by a layer of sticky silt and clay, 0.2m thick, with gravel lenses and tile fragments, perhaps representing a resurfacing. This was sealed by gravelly silt and clay dumps with a high proportion of decayed organic material, filling the sunken area.

Dating: CP1. Cut into the metalling of a Roman street; cut by Building IRO2 (CP2).

Archive ref: IRO80, Period IV.1-IV.3, Building A.

Building IRO2

(Figs 21, 54, 90)

Plan: an oval sunken-floored building, probably 4.2m E-W × 2.8m N-S and 1.1m deep.

First phase

Walls: the impression of an oval earthfast post at the junction of the N and E walls marked the position of a corner post. The impression of a circular post preserved in a contemporary external surface 0.5m from this corner may represent an external wall or roof support.

Internal features: the base of the sunken area was cut by circular feature, 1.8-2.2m in diameter and 0.6m deep. Its base was overlain by thin layer of

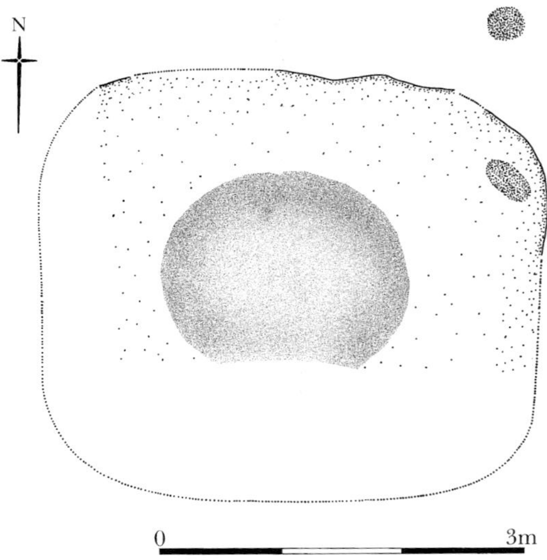

54. Plan of the north-east corner of sunken-floored Structure IRO2. *Note the sunken hearth, and post impressions (shown with heavy stipple).*

silty gravel, sealed by sand and ash mixed with charcoal, showing evidence of *in situ* burning. This may have formed a crude hearth. It was partially backfilled with sandy gravel and sticky pebbly silt tipped down from the W.

Silty gravel accumulated against the sides of the sunken area tipping down into the hearth feature. It was sealed by clean gravel deliberately banked up against the sides of the sunken area to consolidate them. In the N this deposit may have formed rough bedding for timber shoring.

Successive silt and sticky silty clay occupation deposits *c.*0.4m thick accumulated leaving a depression, *c.*1.3m across and up to 0.5m deep, over the earlier hearth which was continually re-cut. These were eventually levelled off with gravelly clay-silt.

Second phase

Walls: the line of the N wall was represented by the impressions of four circular posts, one marking the position of the NE corner.

Internal features: a layer of organic silt represented occpation debris. It was sealed by dumps of gravelly silt and clay with a high organic content.

Dating: CP2. Cut through Building IRO1 (CP1); sealed by Building IRO3 (CP3).

Archive ref: IRO80, Period IV.4-IV.9, Building B.

Building IRO3

(Figs 21, 55)

Plan: the E wall and NE corner of a surface-laid building, at least 3.4m E-W × at least 2.6m N-S.

Walls: the line of the E wall was marked by the impressions of at least four closely-set D-shaped posts set in a slot. These uprights were packed with silt including small tile and ragstone fragments. The N wall-line was marked by a slot of which only a short length survived. Two post impressions at the junction of the N and E wall-lines mark the position of corner posts.

Internal features: an internal surface of silty clay with small chalk fragments.

Dating: CP3. Overlies Building IRO2 (CP2); cut by pits (CP5).

Archive ref: Period V.1-V.2.

55. Plan of the north-east corner of Building IRO3, *which sealed Building* IRO2. *D-shaped impressions for the east wall are shown in black.*

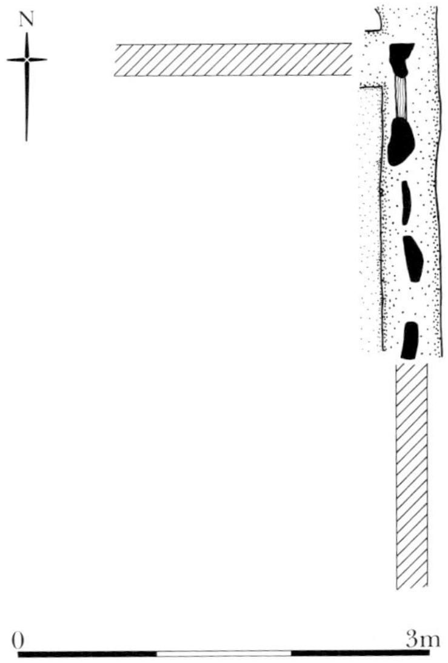

4: THE TIMBER BUILDINGS

Valerie Horsman

Building Types

Some idea of London's early medieval buildings can be gained from the evidence of historical documents, in particular the Assizes of 1189 and 1212. These ordinances were intended to encourage citizens to build in stone rather than wood, in an attempt to contain the frequent fires which had previously destroyed large parts of the City. A particularly spectacular conflagration in 1135 spread from London Bridge to the church of St Clement Danes on the road to Westminster, destroying many buildings including St Paul's. A series of measures to improve the fire-proofing of existing wooden buildings was included in the later Assize and, where citizens were unwilling to comply with these regulations, their houses were demolished (Chew and Kellaway 1973). These documents show that the majority of buildings in the 12th century were of timber construction.

That picture of early medieval London is confirmed by recent excavation and this chapter provides the first detailed assessment of such buildings based solely on archaeological evidence. The data is drawn from the two study areas which together produced evidence of some fifty buildings of 9th to 12th-century date. Five of these buildings were masonry, of which four are considered in a separate publication (Schofield and Allen, forthcoming), but the rest were of timber construction. Although the buildings were by no means as well-preserved as the contemporary examples recently found in York or Dublin, they nevertheless form the largest corpus of such structures in London yet discussed. On a wider level, they provide further useful data to add to the growing body of evidence for Saxon buildings which has accumulated since the last major reviews of this important subject were published (Addyman 1972; Rahtz 1976).

Since the remains of the buildings in London are often slight and usually disturbed by later activity, an understanding of them was only possible after the careful description and drawing of each associated layer and feature. Few of the timbers were left *in situ*, but were removed during demolition, presumably for reuse elsewhere. Aerobic soil conditions hostile to the preservation of wood ensured that any timbers that did remain in the ground were very heavily decayed. Thus, evidence of the superstructure usually survived only in the form of timber impressions, slots or post-holes marking the position of removed or rotted timber. Although examination of these remains has sometimes revealed significant superstructural details, including evidence of the dimensions and shape of wooden components, most of the data relates to the foundations. Nevertheless, a recent study of contemporary structures excavated in York has clearly illustrated that the below-ground elements of early medieval timber buildings can be classified and dated as readily as the superstructures (Addyman 1979, 75).

In London, two main types of building were represented, of which some 60% were of the *surface-laid* type. The remainder were *sunken-floored* structures, a category which includes both outhouses and cellared buildings. In addition, evidence of four timber building traditions has now been identified, in which staves, earth-fast posts, wattlework or timber-retained earth walls are used. Other details recorded concerned partitions, floors, entrances, hearths and ovens, all of which are discussed below.

Surface-laid buildings

(Fig 56)

The remains of 28 surface-laid buildings were recorded, including examples of stave, wattle and post construction. Where the plan could be established, all were rectangular and between 3.2m and 5m wide. The majority were 4 to 5m wide (Milne 1980, 427), as were contemporary structures excavated at Dublin (Murray 1983), York (Hall 1984a, 51, Fig 50) Lincoln (Perring 1981,

Building no.	date	length	width
PEN3	CP2	+1.4m	+3m
PEN12	CP2	+1.8m	c.4m
PEN13	CP3	+1.6m	at least 3.5m
PDN3	CP3	6.4m	c.3.2m
PDN4	CP4	c.7.6m	3.7m
PDN5	CP4	c.10.1m	5m
WEL6	CP4	+6.1m	+4m

measurements refer to external dimensions

56. Sizes of the better-preserved surface-laid buildings.

36), Durham (Carver 1979, 10), Bristol (Rahtz 1976, 411), Thetford (Davison 1967, 192, Figs 44-7, 49), Rhuddlan (Marion Blockley, pers comm; Manley 1987) and Greensted (Christie, Olsen and Taylor 1979, 95).

A much greater degree of variation in length was recorded, ranging from 6.4m to 10.1m, although the full length of very few of the buildings was established. Wattle buildings at Coppergate, York were at least 6.8m long, and were of similar width and construction to the wattle Buildings PEN3, PEN7 and PEN12 in London (Hall 1984a, 51, Fig 48).

Although the full extent of only one structure (PDN3) was preserved, the probable size of two later buildings (PDN4, PDN5) on the same site could be estimated. The smallest of these buildings (PDN3) was 6.4m long by 3.2m wide, the other two, Buildings PDN4 and PDN5, were c.7.6m long by 3.4m wide and c.10.1m long by 5m wide respectively. These three London buildings were therefore approximately twice as long as they were wide. Contemporary buildings whose full extent has been recorded in Dublin and in Rhuddlan in Wales were of similar size to PDN4 (Murray 1983; Marion Blockley, pers comm). The remarkable church of St Andrew at Greensted-juxta-Ongar was in its original form only slightly larger (Christie, Olsen and Taylor 1979, 95).

The majority of the buildings contained only one room. However, evidence of partitions enclosing a second room was recorded in four 9th to 11th-century structures (PEN8, PDN6, PDN4, PDN5), although insufficient of the ground plan of PEN8 and PDN6 survived to determine the precise layout. Building PDN4 was originally an open hall and was subdivided during its second phase. The smaller room, c.1.5m wide, was at the northern end of the building. It occupied the same position as that part of the earlier structure PDN3 which remained in habitation during the construction of PDN4. The function of this smaller room is not known. An extension built onto the northern end wall of the later structure PDN5 acted as a second room. A similar extension on the long wall of contemporary Building L excavated in Thetford was described by the excavator as a kitchen-annexe (Davison 1967, 192;

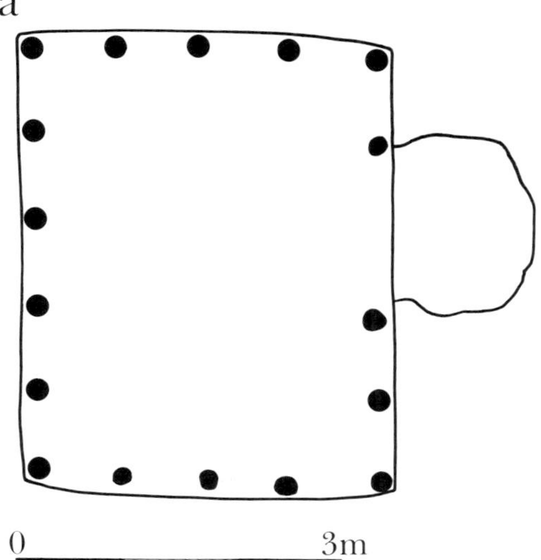

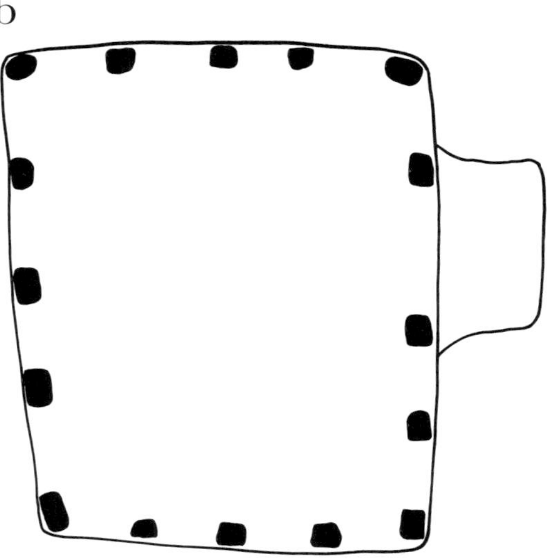

57. Comparative plans of: a) sunken-floored Building MLK1 from London (cf Fig 44); b) a sunken-floored building from Lower Bridge Street, Chester (after Mason 1985).

Fig 57). Like the London building, this second room housed a hearth.

The position of the entrance was identified in only three buildings (PDN3, PDN4, PDN5). Sometimes it was located in a side wall and sometimes on a gable wall. In each example the door opened directly into the living area. In the earliest structures (PDN3, PDN4) the entrance is presumed to have been in the south gable wall (Horsman 1985, 18, 22). Entrances on the gable wall are known from numerous buildings of 9th, 10th and early 11th-century date including examples found in Lincoln (Perring 1981, 7), Dublin (Murray 1983, 33) and Rhuddlan (Marion Blockley, pers comm). In a quite different environment, the entrance to the 9th century farmstead of a small Pennine settlement in Ribblesdale, Yorkshire was also in its gable wall (King 1979, 21).

In the later phase of Building PDN4 and its successor (PDN5), the doorway was in the side wall, entered through a covered porch. The shift in access from the gable to the side wall in Building PDN4 was apparently in response to the demolition of an adjacent building (PDN7). Few examples of doorways in this position are known from contemporary buildings, although some have been found in Dublin, where it is suggested that changes in the position of doors were usually reactions to re-alignments of streets or access to individual properties (Murray 1983, 33).

No evidence was found to suggest that the surface-laid structures were other than domestic buildings. Unfortunately the number of finds from the buildings themselves did not comprise large enough assemblages to facilitate meaningful comparison between building types. The artefacts recovered from these structures and also from the broadly contemporary pits and wells are discussed in *Volume II* (Vince *et al*).

Sunken-floored Buildings

(Fig 58)

Building no.	date	length	width	depth
FMO1	CP1	+3.5m	+2.5m	+0.4m
MLK1	CP1	*c*.4.5m	*c*.3.4m	*c*.1.6m
PDN1	CP2	*c*.5.5m	*c*.3.7m	0.41m
WEL7	CP2-4	*c*.6.5m	+1.8m	+1m
PDN2	CP3	*c*.5.5m	*c*.3.5m	0.41m
PDN11	CP4	*c*.6m	+4.8m	+0.7m
FMO3	CP3	8m	+3.5m	+0.5m
WAT4	CP3	+4.9m	+4.5m	+0.2m
WAT1	CP3	+2.2m	3.6m	*c*.1.2m
WAT3	CP4	*c*.13.4m	*c*.5.4m	2.3m
WAT2	CP4	6.5-12.7m	+5.6m	+0.7m
FMO4	CP4	+9m	+3.5m	+0.5m

measurements refer to external dimensions

58. Table showing the sizes of the better-preserved sunken-floored buildings.

The fragmentary remains of 17 sunken-floored timber buildings were recorded. All incorporated post-and-plank wall construction of which several types were found including, planked wall cladding on both sides of vertical posts and timber-retained earth walls. Post-and-plank construction was used throughout the period from the late 9th to the end of the 11th century (CP1-4), and was by far the most common technique found. Nine of the buildings were rectangular or square in plan but the remaining structures were so fragmentary that their shape could not be ascertained. Where the width of the buildings could be determined it ranged from *c*.2.8m to at least 5.6m and the majority were between 3 and 4m wide. The length varied from 4.2m to 13.4m. The full extent of six buildings (MLK1, PDN1, PDN2, WAT3, IRO1, IRO2) could be determined. All were rectangular or sub-rectangular in plan, but considerable variation was recorded in the size of these structures. The ratio between length and width was calculated for all but one example (IRO1), and varied from 1:1.5 to 1:2.5.

Due to later disturbance of the contemporary ground surface, it was often impossible to determine the original depth below ground level to which the structures penetrated but, where this could be ascertained, it is clear that there was considerable variation. The original depth of eight structures is known (WEL1, MLK1, PDN1, IRO1, IRO2, PDN2, WAT1, WAT3). Although few other construction pits survived to their original depth, many of the buildings may have been set as deep as contemporary buildings of a similar size found in Canterbury, Chester, Oxford and York where depths of 1.6m-1.8m have been recorded. However, several of the London buildings (eg PDN1, PDN2) were exceptionally shallow, penetrating only 0.41m below the ground surface while Building WAT3 was up to 2.3m deep.

The widely-varying depths of these structures is one of a number of characteristics which suggests, though does not prove, that the sunken-floored buildings were of different structural types, some being of one and some of two stories. Taken on its own, the depth below ground-level of the sunken area need not necessarily suggest that a building was more than one storey high. Indeed structures which penetrated to a depth of 1.7m below the ground surface have been interpreted as one-storey buildings in York (Hall 1984b, 75), and as two-storey buildings in Chester (Mason 1985, 20). Other relevant criteria must therefore be considered, including the width of posts supporting the walls and the presence of hearths.

It is unlikely that posts of less than 0.2m (8 inches) in cross-section could have supported a second storey. Unfortunately the dimensions of the posts are often not known as only the post-holes remain, and in those examples where baseplates were used to support the wall-posts (eg PDN1-2, WEL7) it is of course impossible to assess the size of associated vertical members. Nevertheless, on the basis that posts of 0.2m diameter or larger were used, several of the London structures may have been cellared buildings supporting a second storey at ground level (see Fig 79). This category includes Building MLK1, which was exceptional in that it had a hearth on its floor surface. However, since it is unlikely that an open hearth would have been practical in the basement of a wooden structure with an upper storey, it is suggested that Building MLK1 would not have had two stories. Building MLK1 was almost identical in plan to contemporary Structures 3 and 4 excavated on the Lower Bridge Street site in Chester (Fig 57).

It would therefore seem that, with one or two exceptions, the sunken-floored structures found in London represent three quite different types of contemporary building, although it must be admitted that the distinctions between the proposed categories are by no means clear cut. Again, the study of finds directly associated with these structures has not helped to establish differences in function (see *Volume II*). Nevertheless, three main types may be summarised thus:

59. Remains of large cellared Building WAT3 *cut by later wells and pits, looking north. The 10 × 100mm scales rest on the internal surface, with the line of the east wall visible to the west of the modern foundations.*

Sunken-floored outhouses

Some characteristics of this type of building would seem to include relatively modest proportions, a floor set less than 1m below ground surface, major load-bearing timbers of less than 0.2m in diameter, and the presence of open hearths. Such structures may well have been used for workshops, temporary accommodation or storage, and are generally interpreted as outhouses complementary to, but not structurally integrated with, a principal range. They were usually situated in the back yard area of a property (see p.108), or at least well away from the street frontage (eg IRO1, IRO2).

Sunken-floored buildings

At least two examples of this type of building have been recorded (MLK1, PDN11). They were sunk up to 1.5m below the contemporary ground surface and were larger than the outhouses just described. The recording of resurfacing and hearths afforded clear evidence of occupation, and this contrasts significantly with the cellared buildings (see below). It is possible that Buildings PDN1 and 2 were more modest versions of this type.

Cellared buildings

(Fig 59)

A third type of sunken-floored building was identified, of which at least five examples were recorded (FMO1, FMO2, WAT1, WAT2, WAT3). They were more substantial structures, deeply-set below the ground level, with no evidence of hearths. As such, they are thought to represent the sub-surface element of buildings which also had a room or rooms at ground level. It is presumed that the lower section of these buildings was used for storage as a cellar. Since no examples of partitions were recorded, it seems that the cellars were one-roomed structures. Such cellared buildings may well have been structurally-integrated with the principal range, although they are frequently found at the rear of the buildings which are presumed to have lain against the street frontage itself (see p.109).

5: STRUCTURAL DETAILS

Valerie Horsman

In this section, foundation and wall construction details recorded from the two study areas are discussed and compared with better-preserved examples from elsewhere in Britain. No direct evidence of roof construction was recorded on the London sites, but a short consideration of this topic is included in Part 7.

Foundations

(Fig 60)

Although the walls of the Saxo-Norman buildings had often been dismantled, the remains of the foundations were often relatively well-preserved. Evidence of the wall foundations of 28 timber building was recorded and classified into three main types, *earthfast*, *floor and ground-level*, and *foundation-bed*, as shown in Figs 13, 56, 58, 60. The foundation beds were first used in the period between the mid-10th to early 11th-century (CP2); the other two types of foundation were in use from the late 9th to the late 11th century (CP1-4).

Date	earthfast	floor and ground-level	foundation bed
CP1	FMO1*		
	MLK1*	MLK1*	
	PEN9		
			PDN1*
CP2	PEN12	IRO2*	
	MLK4		
	FMO2*		
	PEN6		
			PDN2*
CP3	WAT1*		
	PDN6	PDN3	PDN3
	IRO3		
	PEN13		
	WEL3		
	WEL5		
	PDN11*		
		WAT3*	PDN7
CP4	WAT3*	PDN8	PDN4
	PDN8		PDN5
	WEL6		
	WAT2*		
			WEL7*
CP5	PDN9		

(* = sunken-floored structure)

60. Foundation types.

Earthfast foundations

(Figs 61a, 62)

The majority of the buildings under discussion had earthfast foundations, and these included both sunken-floored and surface-laid structures. Several methods of construction were employed including baseplates laid in slots; stakes driven into the ground surface; vertical posts set in individual postholes (often packed with rubble); and vertical posts set at intervals in shallow slots, a technique known as 'post-in-trench'. The last technique allows a more accurate alignment of the upright posts than is possible using individual postholes or driven stakes. It is therefore considered by some to be a more 'advanced' technique (Rahtz 1976, 84). In London, walls with individual postholes continued to be erected long after the introduction of the post-in-trench techniques. Often both methods were employed in the same structure, as in Buildings WEL3, WAT1, MLK4. Similarily, two walls of Building FMO1 exhibited different techniques, with the west wall incorporating a baseplate laid within a slot, and the north wall comprising a line of earthfast posts set in individual postholes.

Floor and ground-level construction

(Figs 61b, 63)

Examples of this technique were only recorded in

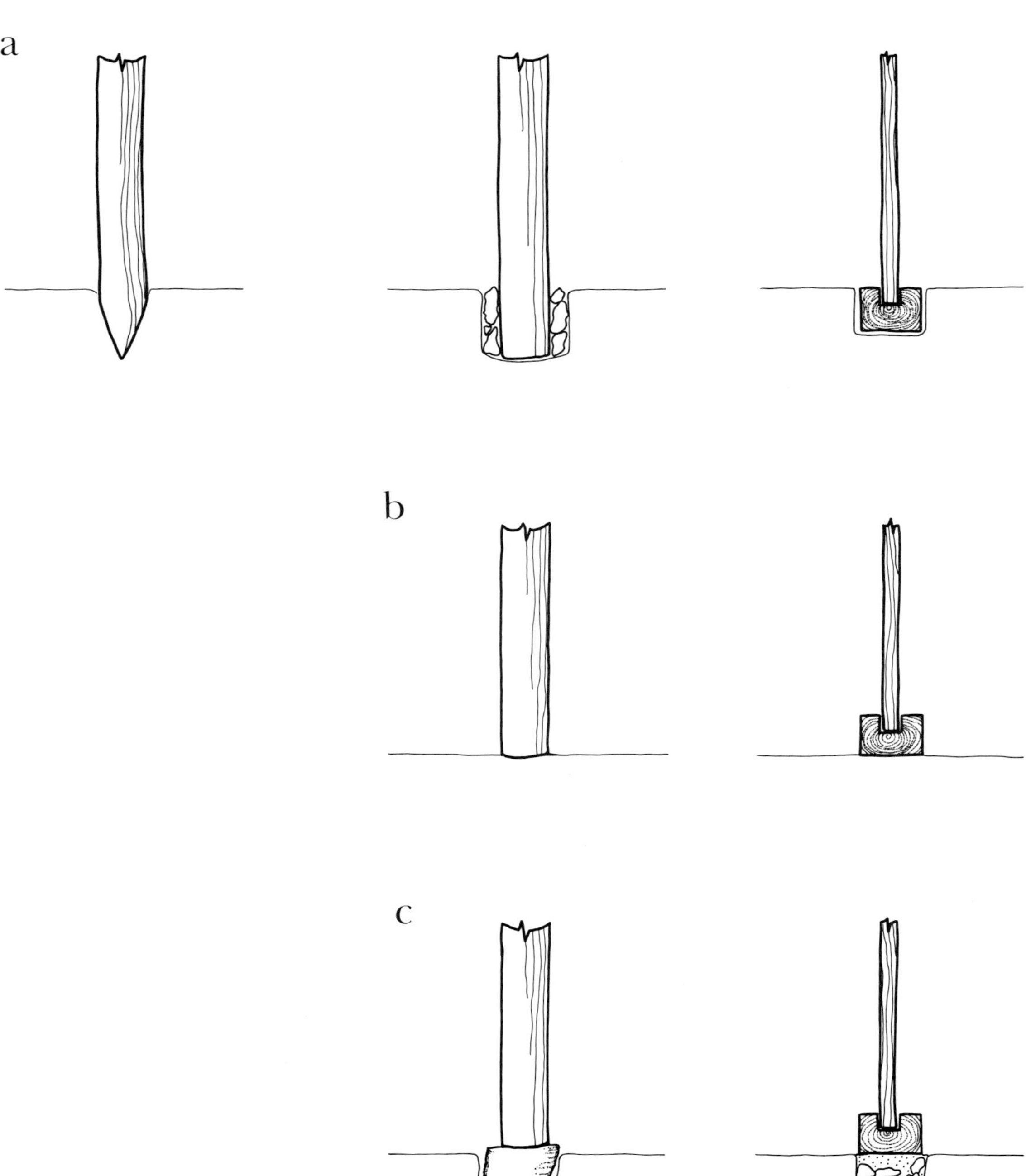

five structures. Foundation beams resting directly on the ground surface were found in two surface-laid buildings (PDN3, PDN8). In three sunken-floored structures (MLK1, WAT3, PDN8) which had at least one wall of earthfast construction, post impressions showed that one other wall simply rested on the sunken floor surface.

61. Sections to show the three main types of timber wall foundations: a) earthfast; b) ground level; c) foundation bed.

Foundation beds

(Figs 61c, 64)

Examples of walls supported on foundation beds

Date	posthole	stakehole	baseplate-in-slot	post-in-trench
CP1	FMO1*		FMO1*	
	MLK1*			
	PEN9			
		PEN12		MLK4
CP2	MLK4			FMO2*
	PEN6			
		PEN13		WAT1
CP3	WAT1*			IRO3
	PDN6			WEL3
	WEL3			
		PDN8		WAT2*
CP4	WAT3*			PDN11*
	WEL5			WEL6
CP5	PDN9			

(* = sunken-floored structure)

62. Methods of earthfast construction.

Date	foundation beam	vertical post
CP1		MLK1*
CP2		IRO2*
CP3	PDN3	
CP4	PDN8	WAT3*
CP5		

(* = sunken-floored building)

63. Types of floor and ground-level foundation.

Date	levelled padstones	clay and rubble	mortar-packed trench
CP1			
CP2	PDN1*		
CP3	PDN2*		
	PDN3		
CP4	PDN4	WEL7*	PDN4
			PDN7
			PDN5

(* = sunken-floored structure)

64. Types of foundation bed.

accounted for slightly less than a third of the structures for which evidence of the foundations survived, and were recorded in both sunken-floored and surface-laid structures. With the exception of Building WEL7, all the examples were part of the same sequence of sunken-floored and surface-laid buildings (PDN1-5). This sequence is especially interesting since PDN3-5 represent phases of one property modified and enlarged over a considerable period of time (Fig 65). Three types of foundation bed were found; the first utilised rows of levelled padstones, sometimes with small timbers; the second, a compacted clay/silt and rubble platform; and finally, a mortar-capped trench packed with chalk, ragstone rubble, or sand and gravel.

Rows of levelled padstones supported the walls of sunken-floored Buildings PDN1-3 (Fig 66). In the earlier sunken-floored buildings, the padstones rested on the base of the sunken area. By contrast, the padstones for the walls of the later surface-laid Building PDN3 were laid in shallow slots. On the east wall the slot gave way to small timber chocks laid on the ground surface. Various materials were used including fragments of red Roman tile, limestone, ragstones, whole and fragmented quern stones. The querns were in an unfinished condition and all but one were of Niedermendig lava stone imported from Germany. Padstones were often used to raise vertical posts above the ground to prevent damp decay but the levelled surface of London foundations indicates that they supported baseplates not individual posts. Only the east, west and north walls of PDN3 were raised above the ground in this way, the south wall resting directly on the ground surface. Significantly, those walls supported on foundations were built on top of redeposited soil, infilling the sunken area of the earlier Building PDN2, demolished before Building PDN3 was built. By contrast, the south wall of Building PDN3 was erected on firmer ground undisturbed by earlier activity. This would suggest that the foundations were introduced primarily to provide a stable base for the building, rather than to protect the timber superstructure from damp decay.

A foundation comprising a clay and rubble-packed trench was discovered in sunken-floored Building WEL7, over which traces of a timber baseplate were recorded. A similar technique using different materials was used to support the

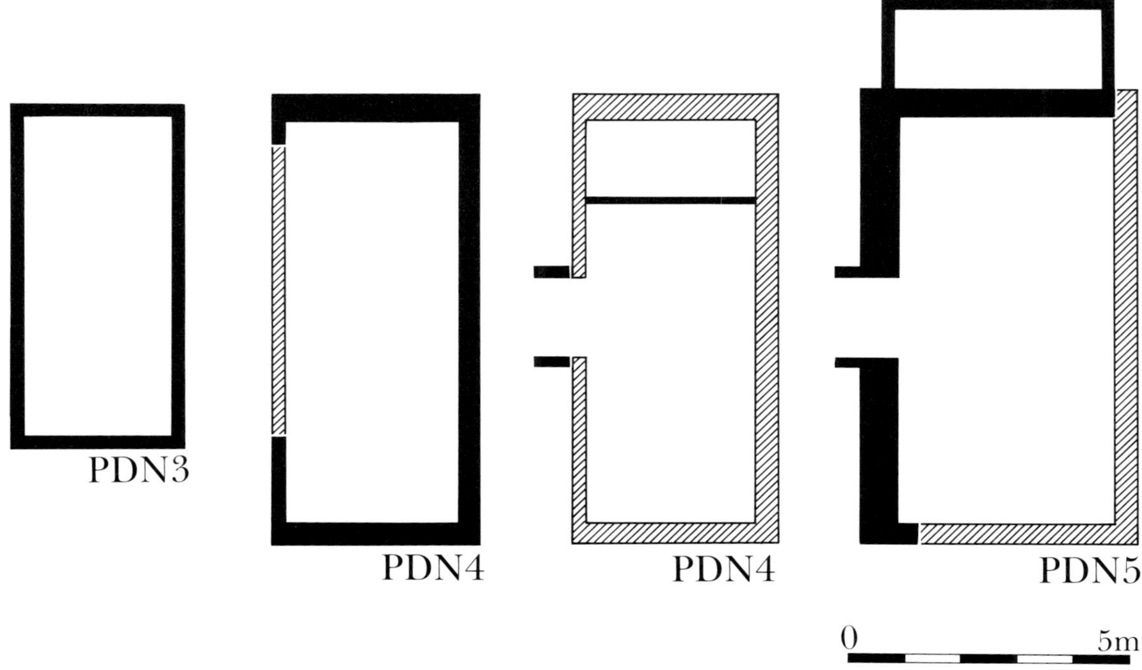

walls of the three surface-laid Buildings PDN4, PDN5, PDN7. After Building PDN7 was dismantled the foundation for its east wall was used to support the west wall of an extension to Building PDN5. The simplest foundation, supporting the west wall of Building PDN7, consisted of a shallow slot packed with mortar (Fig 67). The walls of Buildings PDN4 and 5 were supported on crushed mortar beds laid over deep trenches filled with gravel and sand, or ragstone and chalk rubble (Fig 68). A curious feature of the foundation for the east wall of Building PDN4 was the remains of several charred and decayed planks sandwiched between the gravel and mortar trench fills (Fig 69). These had no structural function. The trenches themselves were not uniform in size but the greater depth and width of the foundations supporting the west wall and north-west corner of the later Building PDN5 probably reflects attempts to prevent subsidence resulting from construction along a line of earlier pits and wells.

The technique of supporting the walls on trenches filled with crushed mortar or rubble is also known from the Saxon church of St Botolph in Hadstock, Essex (Rodwell 1976, 60), a contemporary building excavated in High Ousegate, York (Radley 1971, 42), and a hall found beneath Waltham Abbey, similarly dated to the 11th century (Huggins 1976, 86). A slightly different

65. Plan showing the development of Buildings PDN3-5. Wall lines thought to have been built at each phase are shown in black; walls retained from a previous structure are shown hatched. Building PDN4 represents substantial modifications to Building PDN3, while Building PDN5 represents substantial modifications to a later phase of Building PDN4 (cf Figs 25, 30, 32, 36.

example of the same technique is provided by a lime cement pad at St Paul's Hall, Belchamp St Paul, Essex, which supported a post with a radiocarbon date of 1026 AD +/- 95 years (Hewett 1980, 23).

The use of mortar chalk and ragstone rubble-filled trenches, albeit as the foundations for timber buildings, indicates an increasing awareness of the techniques of masonry construction in London by the early to mid-11th century (CP3). Indeed, it is suggested that the materials were not specially imported but probably obtained from a nearby site on which a stone building was being erected. Similar to the foundations of the timber buildings, but significantly wider and deeper, were the foundations of the 12th-century stone Building PDN10 (CP5). A similar contrast in size was observed between stone foundations of pre- and post-Conquest buildings in York (Addyman 1979, 71).

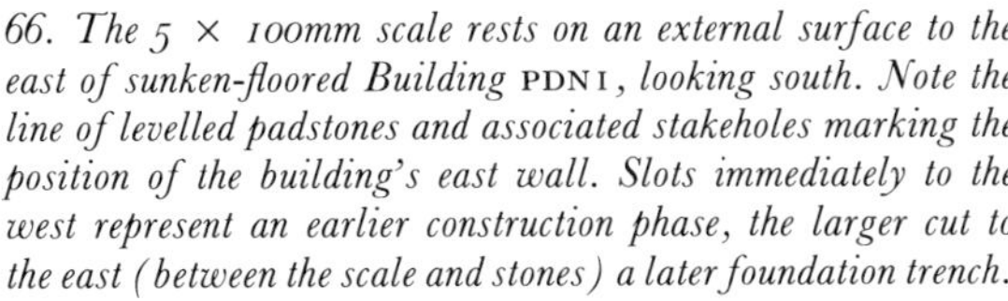

66. The 5 × 100mm scale rests on an external surface to the east of sunken-floored Building PDN1, *looking south. Note the line of levelled padstones and associated stakeholes marking the position of the building's east wall. Slots immediately to the west represent an earlier construction phase, the larger cut to the east (between the scale and stones) a later foundation trench.*

67. Eastern half of Building PDN4, looking south. The 5 × *100mm scale rests on the internal surface, with the 2 × 100mm scale on the mortar-capped foundation of the east wall. Although the timber baseplate has been removed, its position is marked by the western edge of the patch of earth packing visible on the surface of the foundation, just north-east of 0.5m scale.*

Wall Construction

(Fig 70)

It now seems that there were at least four principal methods in use from the late 9th to the late 11th century (CP1-4), incorporating *staves*, *posts*, *wattlework*, and *timber-retained earth*.

Stave-building

(Fig 70a)

Stave-building first appears in London in the 11th century (CP3), and has been found incorporated in waterfront embankments as well as in the contemporary buildings. Two examples are known from dry-land sites, one of which employed an earthfast stave wall, the other a stave wall set in a baseplate. The earthfast stave wall was recorded in Building IRO3 (p.65), and comprised D-shaped timbers alternated with thinner planks set in a narrow trench. An initial assessment of the remains of Building IRO3 suggested that the staves had been supported by a wooden baseplate (Norton 1982, 175). Subsequent analysis of the evidence, however, suggests that the staves were set earthfast. The D-shaped posts, *c.*0.36m by 0.1-0.16m in size may have been tree trunks split in half, similar to those still forming the walls of the

68. The north-west corner of Buildings PDN4 *and 5 disturbed by modern concrete and brick foundations, looking east. The 2 × 100mm scale rests on the chalk rubble foundation (*PDN5*) abutting the remains of mortar foundation to east (*PDN4*).*

69. Construction of Building PDN4*, looking south. The 5 × 100mm scale rests on the internal surface, with the 2 × 100mm scale on the remains of charred planks within the east wall foundation.*

church of St Andrew, Greensted-juxta-Ongar, Essex, (Christie, Olsen and Taylor 1979, 97). Their curved surfaces, like the Greensted examples, was on the outside. The NE corner of IRO3 was formed by two smaller rectangular posts. No evidence for any jointing survived. Better-preserved earthfast stave buildings of late Saxon date have been found at Rhuddlan in Wales (Blockley forthcoming), and earlier examples of the technique are known from Goltho, in Lincolnshire (Beresford 1982, 114; Fig 6.1). The use of alternate thin and thicker staves in the wall is a type of construction known from Building CP85/i, an 11th-century structure found in Dublin (Murray 1983, 27-8) and from a church at Urnes in Norway usually dated *c.*1060 (Murray 1983, 29).

Building PDN3 (p.39) incorporated stave walls set in a baseplate, of which two sections were preserved. A narrow longitudinal groove cut in the centre of their upper surface provided evidence of the use of vertically-set staves (Horsman 1985, 19). At the junction of the south and east walls, the only corner which survived, the baseplates abutted each other, apparently without any jointing. No evidence for a corner post survived. The east wall baseplate was formed of at least two dressed timbers. Better-preserved contemporary examples of stave-in-baseplate construction were uncovered during the excavation of waterfront embankments in the Saxon harbour near Billingsgate in 1983 (Fig 71). In addition, staves derived from a dismantled building were reused in an early 13th-century revetment found on this site (Horsman 1985, 20).

Contemporary examples of stave-in-baseplate construction are known from Dublin (Murray 1983, 27), while a grooved baseplate similar to that recorded in the London Building PDN3 has been found in York (Addyman 1979, 70), but this structure incorporated earthfast corner posts.

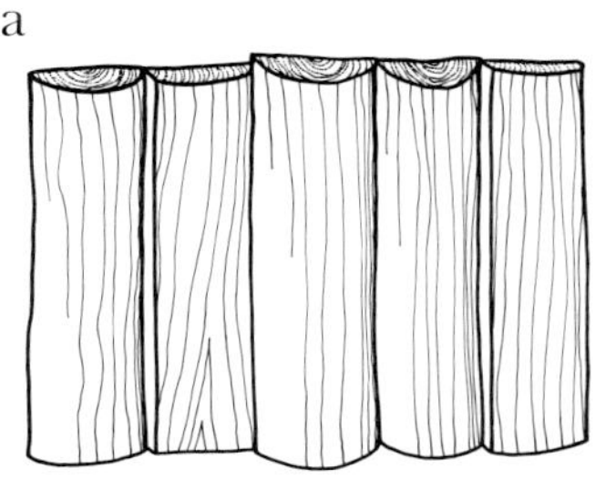

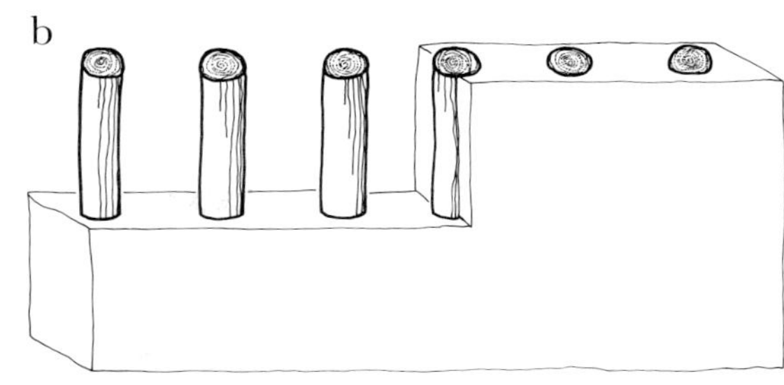

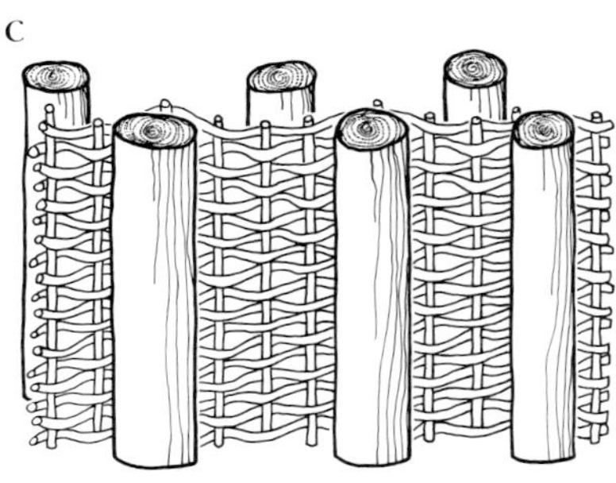

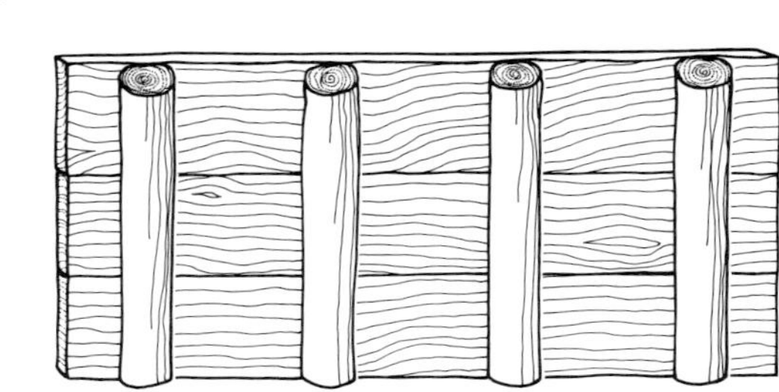

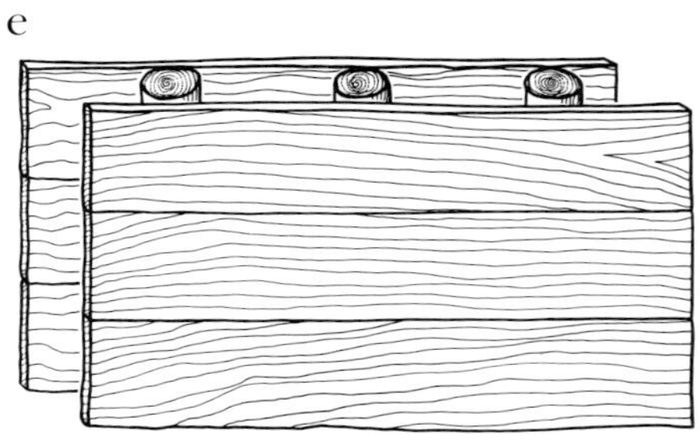

f

70. Elevations to show the main types of wall construction: a) stave building; b) post in earth wall; c) paired post and wattle; d) post with cladding on outer face; e) post with plank cladding on inner and outer face; f) planks set in vertically-grooved posts.

Excavations by Richard Bluer on the Sunlight Wharf site in London in 1987 uncovered a 12th or early 13th-century riverfront revetment with staves set in a baseplate which also incorporated some earthfast elements (Richard Bluer, pers comm).

Earthfast posts

(Fig 61a)

A more common method of wall construction in Saxon London employed earthfast posts. The fragmentary remains of 15 such buildings were excavated, and ranged in date from the late 9th to the early 12th century (CP1-4). It was possible to identify specific details of wall construction in several of these examples. The techniques of *post-and-mud* and *paired post-and-wattle* wall-construction were only employed in the surface-laid buildings (Fig 70b, c).

The west wall of Building WEL3 (p. 61) incorp-

orated a wattle framework set within a double row of parallel posts erected at irregular intervals in a shallow trench (Fig 72). Better-preserved remains of buildings of this type are known from Dublin, where the wattlework was sandwiched between earthfast planks set at regular intervals (Murray 1983, 26, Fig 40).

In London, part of the west wall of Building WEL6 (p.62) had been built of circular posts 0.11m thick, probably encased within a earthern wall-cladding at least 0.2m wide. The wall posts were erected 0.7m apart in a shallow trench, their bases secured with rubble packing (Fig 73). The better-preserved remains of more substantial buildings of this type have been found at Goltho in Lincolnshire (Beresford 1982, 119; Fig 6.5). The walls of the Goltho examples were usually between 0.38m and 0.53m thick, strengthened by vertical unsawn posts up to 0.23m in diameter set at regular intervals of 0.9m.

Seven examples of *post-and plank* walled structures were recorded in London, all from sunken-floored buildings (MLK1, FMO1, FMO2, WAT1, WAT2, WAT3, PDN11). Sometimes the plank cladding was attached to the outer face of the post, occasionally on both faces, and sometimes the

71. Billingsgate Lorry Park excavations, 1982-3, looking north-east. The 5 × 100mm scale rests on the foreshore to the south of an 11th-century stave-built waterfront structure set in a grooved baseplate (BIG82).

planks were set into vertical grooves cut in the edges of upright posts.

The remains of three structures (MLK1, FMO1, FMO2) with evidence of an outer plank-face were found (Fig 70d). The walls of the best-preserved example, Building MLK1 (p.52), were built of posts 0.2m thick supporting an external face of planks set edge on edge. The posts were set 0.8m apart around the base of the sunken area: those on the southern wall were earthfast and those on the east wall stood on the internal surface.

By contrast, the planked north wall of Buildings FMO1 and FMO2 (p.50) was supported by large closely-set earthfast posts of varying cross-section. The planked cladding itself was removed but an impression of the timber remained between the line of posts and the side of the sunken area. The wall posts were set in rubble-packed postholes, 0.5m deep, dug at irregular intervals into a narrow earthen platform preserved 0.2m above the base of the sunken area. The west wall of the

72. West wall of Building WEL3, *looking north. The 2 × 100mm scale rests in a foundation trench in which paired posts either side of a wattle wall were represented.*

73. West wall of Building WEL6, *looking north, with 10 × 10mm scale. The traces of the post and wattle wall can be clearly seen.*

earlier Building FMO1 was supported on a baseplate set in a shallow slot. A similar method of construction was apparently used to build the substantial timber structure on the southern foreshore of the Thames excavated by George Dennis in 1984. That timber structure was sealed beneath part of the late 12th-century London Bridge, and may have been associated with the late Saxon Bridge.

Other structures employing this technique are known from London (Grimes 1968, 155-7) and other towns including, Canterbury (Webster and Cherry 1980, 225-6), Chester (Mason 1985, 20), Ipswich (Young and Clark 1985, 200), Oxford (Hassall 1974-5, 39-40) Wallingford (Durham 1980, 44) and York (Hall 1982, 238-40). The best-preserved examples are provided by the late 10th and 11th-century sunken-floored structures excavated at Coppergate, York.

Planked wall cladding on both sides of vertical posts (Fig 70e) is known from two 11th-century structures in London, Buildings WAT2 and WAT3 (p.56). The walls were constructed of dressed upright posts, *c.*0.2m square, clad inside and out with planks laid edge-on-edge (Figs 74-5). It is suggested that the cavity was then packed with silt to form a solid wall, although it has been argued elsewhere that the cavity may have been left empty (Perring 1982, 211). The vertical posts in each structure were set at regular intervals of 1m and 0.9m respectively. The remains of other late 10th and 11th-century structures with planked walls of this type have been found on the Cannon Street site in London (Grimes 1968, 157; Fig 35) and on Coppergate in York (Hall 1982, 239; Fig 13.5). Unlike WAT2 and WAT3, the cavity plank walls of the York example were not apparently infilled. Evidence of this general type of wall construction has also been found in contemporary structures excavated in Dublin (Murray 1983, 23-26), where the walls were built of an inner and outer skin of wattles. In common with the London buildings, the cavity was infilled (Murray 1983, 25).

74. Detail of cellared Building WAT2 *cut by a modern brick foundation. To the left of the 5 × 100mm scale are the impressions of the post and plank-clad walls.*

75. East wall of cellared Building WAT3, *with the 5 × 100mm scale outside it. The 2 × 100mm scale is on the internal surface next to a line of voids marking a wall built from regularly-spaced squared posts clad internally and externally with planking.*

The possibility that the walls of Buildings MLK1, FMO1 and FMO2 originally incorporated an inner skin of planking, like the later Buildings WAT2 and WAT3, cannot be excluded. The regular spacing of the wall posts of the post-and-plank Buildings MLK1, WAT2 and WAT3 probably reflects the position of parallel posts supporting the opposite wall. Such pairing was recorded in buildings of a similar type found elsewhere in London (Grimes 1968, 158; Fig 35), in York (Hall 1982, 239) and in Chester (Mason 1985, figs 8, 10). The spacing between the wall posts of the London and Chester buildings was in considerable contrast to the buildings at Coppergate, where the posts were closely-set at intervals of only 0.3m (Hall 1984, 71).

The planked walls of the London buildings were occasionally set directly against the edges of the sunken area and sometimes just inside them, when the intervening space was packed with clay. In this way, outward movement of the plank boarding was prevented. The planks forming the external face of the walls may therefore, like the Coppergate buildings, have simply been wedged between the posts and the soil (Hall 1982, 239; Hall 1984a, 270). The greater amount of wood consumed in the construction of the double-faced plank walls suggests these structures would have been more expensive to build than those with a single plank face. The clay packing filling the cavity between the plank faces of these London buildings would have provided effective damp-proofing, essential if the lower storey was used as a cellar.

Baseplates were used to support the walls of Building WAT3, and, although the timber was heavily decayed, it is clear that the northern baseplate had an inner shoulder to retain the feet of the posts. It is not known whether the vertical posts rested on the baseplates or were set into them. In York, baseplates with an inner shoulder supported walls of the late 10th-century sunken-

floored structures found at Coppergate (Hall 1982, 238).

In contrast to Buildings WAT2 and 3, the walls of Hut Pit 2 at Cannon Street were built of deeply-set earthfast posts erected at 1.1m intervals along a narrow gully or sleeper trench. From the published plan of the structure it appears that the posts were separated by lengths of baseplate (Grimes 1968, 157; Fig 35). This 'interupted-sill-beam' technique has not been found in buildings of this type elsewhere in London but is known in York from an Anglo-Scandinavian building found on a site at 6/8 Pavement (Addyman 1974, 221) and from the mid-10th-century long hall excavated at Goltho (Beresford 1982, 119; Fig 6.4). However, evidence of this type of construction was found in London during recent excavation of a 12th or 13th-century riverfront revetment recorded on the Sunlight Wharf site in 1987 (Richard Bluer pers comm).

Another technique, using *planks set in vertical grooves* cut in the edges of upright posts (Figs 70f, 76), was recorded in the 11th-century Building PDN11 (CP3-4: see p.50). The planks were preserved as traces of woodstain on the side of the sunken area. The pattern of corroded ironwork

76. Sunken-floored Building PDN11, much disturbed by later brick and masonry features, looking south-west. The 5 × 100mm scale sits in an intrusion cut through the internal brick-earth floor of the building. Marking the northern and eastern edges of that surface are the remains of the post-supported walls.

within the woodstain revealed that some of the timbers were reused strakes from a partially dismantled boat. Posts with vertical grooves were found in 12th or 13th-century waterfront structures on the Seal House (Schofield 1975) and Baynard Castle sites (Marsden et al. 1975, 188; Fig 8). The same technique of construction was used to build 11th-century timber-lined wells on the Pudding Lane (Fig 77) and nearby Triangle sites (Jones 1980, 14, Figs 8 and 9).

Timber-retained earth walls were used in the sunken-floored structures PDN1 PDN2 (pp.37, 38-9; Fig 98). It is suggested that that the walls were built of earth upcast during excavation of the sunken area. The earth was probably piled behind a wooden framework retained by stakes and supported on levelled rows of padstones laid on the base of the sunken area.

Buildings of this type are known from the Cannon Street site in London, where traces of a

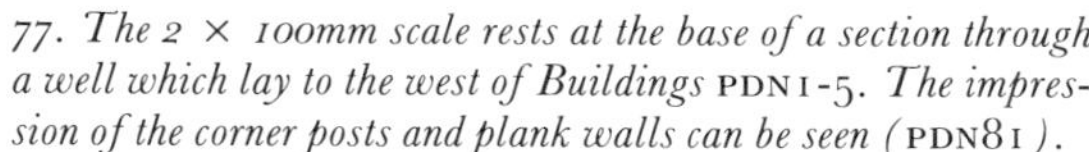

77. *The 2 × 100mm scale rests at the base of a section through a well which lay to the west of Buildings* PDN1-5. *The impression of the corner posts and plank walls can be seen (*PDN81*).*

78. *Billingsgate Lorry Park excavation, 1982-3. The 2 × 100mm scale rests on a collapsed wattlework structure used to retain the 11th-century waterfront embankment (*BIG82*).*

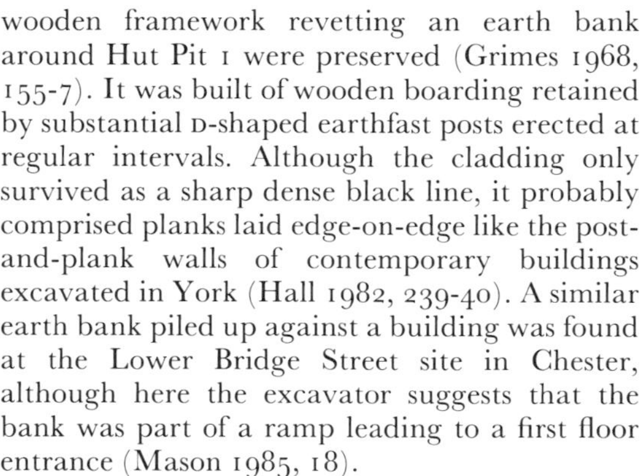

wooden framework revetting an earth bank around Hut Pit 1 were preserved (Grimes 1968, 155-7). It was built of wooden boarding retained by substantial D-shaped earthfast posts erected at regular intervals. Although the cladding only survived as a sharp dense black line, it probably comprised planks laid edge-on-edge like the post-and-plank walls of contemporary buildings excavated in York (Hall 1982, 239-40). A similar earth bank piled up against a building was found at the Lower Bridge Street site in Chester, although here the excavator suggests that the bank was part of a ramp leading to a first floor entrance (Mason 1985, 18).

Wattlework

(Fig 70c)

Wattle buildings were relatively uncommon. Evidence of the use of this technique was found in five surface-laid structures ranging in date from the 10th to the 12th century. Two variations in the method of construction were identified, one of which used earthfast wattles, the other wattles supported on a baseplate.

The fragmentary remains of *earthfast wattlework* was found in three structures (PEN12, PEN13, PDN8) with walls built of withies interwoven with earthfast stakes. Although traces of the interwoven withies were preserved in only one example (PDN8, p.48), the regular spacing and uniform size of stakeholes marking the wall-lines of Buildings PEN12 and PEN13 (p.36) indicated the use of a similar wattle superstructure. Although few buildings of wattle construction have been found in London (eg Chitwood 1983), the technique was evidently well known, as the discovery of wattle hurdles on the 10th/11th-century bank at Billingsgate and numerous wattle pit linings at Milk Street and other London sites attest (Fig 78). Better-preserved examples of contemporary wattle buildings are known from York (Hall 1982,

Building no.	date	timber	dimensions	cross-section
MLK1	CP1	wall posts planks	c.0.2m in diam	rounded
FMO1	CP1	wall posts	**	D-shaped rect D-shaped
IRO3	CP3	staves	0.34m × c.0.15m 0.3m × 80mm	rect
PDN3	CP3	E & W baseplates	0.24m wide × at least 0.12m thick (with longitudinal groove on top face)	rect
PDN4	4	baseplate	c.0.25m sq.	
PDN8	CP4	baseplate	c.0.24m wide × at least 40mm thick	
WAT2	CP4	wall posts	c.0.2m sq.	squared
WAT3	CP4	E baseplate	c.0.24m sq.	
		N baseplate	c.0.27m wide, with inner shoulder	
		wall posts	c.0.2m sq.	squared
		planks	c.50mm thick	

79. Timberworking details.

234-8), Durham (Carver 1979) and Dublin (Murray 1983, 19-23).

The technique of wall construction using *wattles supported on a foundation beam* was recorded in Buildings PDN8 and PDN9 (p.48). Evidence of the wattlework survived only as impressions in fragments of burnt daub thought to have originally coated the walls. The carbonised remains of part of the baseplate supporting the south wall of the later example (PDN9) was preserved, but only an impression of the baseplate carrying the east wall of Building PDN8 remained. Both had been laid flat. No evidence of the inter-relationship between the baseplates and the wattle and daub superstructure remained.

Other examples of this technique are known from York, Dublin, Aberdeen and Perth. In York, the rear wall of a 10th-century wattle building was built in this fashion but, unlike the London examples, the baseplate was set on edge (Hall 1982, 237-8). In Perth and Aberdeen, buildings of similar construction to the London examples, but later date, have been found (Blanchard 1980, 34-6; Figs 2-3; Murray 1980, 39, 41-2). In Dublin, internal partitions subdividing an 11th-century stave-built structure were built in this fashion (Murray 1983, 26, 131-2; Fig 55).

Timberworking

(Fig 79)

The little evidence relating to timberworking practice that was recorded is shown in Fig 79. Although the lower face and inside edges of these baseplates were apparently flat, the outer edge of one example (PDN4) was curved, showing that not all of the faces had been squared. From the limited evidence available, it could be suggested that, with the exception of the D-shaped timbers, dressed posts and baseplates of roughly similar size were used. Although the timbers were too heavily decayed for species identification it is assumed that they were oak. According to normal yield tables produced by the Forestry Commission, oak posts with a diameter of 0.2m would have been cut from trees at least 45 years old (Forestry Commission Booklet no. 16, 200; table 67), while the baseplates could have been prepared from trees between 55 and 65 years old.

Earthfast and floor and ground-level construction

The range of wall and foundation-types recorded in London is clearly significant, and merits comment. The rigidity of the earthfast buildings was achieved by securing the bases of the walls in the ground rather than relying on the structural integration of the wooden framework. By contrast, the stability of buildings whose walls rested on the floor surface or were supported on foundation beds, required a greater integration of the superstructure. However, there was no evidence from London to suggest that one technique gradually superceded the other. On the contrary, examples of structures were discovered in which earthfast foundations were incorporated with timbers set directly upon the floor surface or on foundation beds. Such buildings required a greater degree of integration than those solely employing the technique of earthfast construction. What is certain is that buildings which were constructed with timbers set earthfast, or at floor and ground-level, or on specially-built foundation-beds clearly co-existed in London from the 10th to the 12th centuries. At the manorial site in Wintringham, Huntingdonshire, the use of a similar range of techniques reflected the differing status and function of the excavated buildings, which included a hall, kitchen and bower (Beresford 1977, 226, Table 1). In conclusion it can be said that little has been found in London to suggest that the development of structurally-integrated buildings resting on the floor or the ground surface or on foundation beds led directly to the replacement of the more 'primitive' buildings of earthfast construction, as has been suggested elsewhere (Rahtz 1976, 93-4).

6: FLOORS, DOORS AND INTERNAL FEATURES

Valerie Horsman

Floors

(Figs 80,81-83)

Evidence of eight different types of flooring was preserved in 35 of the timber buildings excavated. They included beaten-earth, clay/brickearth, crushed chalk, gravel, mortar, sand, wood, grass or rushes. There was no evidence that different types of floor were related to the function of the building. The beaten-earth, clay/brickearth, crushed chalk, gravel, mortar and sand floors were formed from thick slabs or bands of material often repaired and resurfaced. Floors of similar construction are known from early medieval buildings found in Lincoln, Chester, York, Thetford and Dublin.

By far the most common flooring in London was beaten-earth although brickearth was extensively used, except in the 11th century (CP3). Relatively little evidence of sand or grassy floors was found, unlike Lincoln where floors of these type predominated (Perring 1981, 39). The occasional use of sand and gravel did not appear to signify any special function. The absence of beaten-earth floors from Buildings PDN4, PDN5 is notable and in marked contrast to other buildings. Floors within these two buildings included materials such as chalk, mortar and sand, materials which were rarely used elsewhere. Although the use of these materials may be related to the status of the buildings, it more probably simply reflects their availability: the foundations of both buildings were also constructed of chalk, mortar and sand. With the exception of the planked floors, whose use was confined to the sunken-floored structures discussed below, there was no other evident difference between the types of flooring employed in sunken or surface-laid buildings.

Evidence of wooden floors was found in two sunken-floored buildings (PDN1, WAT3), although in neither case was the planking forming the floor preserved. The floor of the earlier structure (PDN1) apparently rested on widely-spaced planks set on edge and positioned immediately inside the walls, but the supports themselves had been removed when a later beaten-earth floor was laid. By contrast, D-shaped wooden joists running the length of the building supported the floor of the later Building WAT3 (see Fig 23). These joists were set flat-face down in shallow slots, their upper surface protruding 0.1m above the ground. The underfloor cavities thus created would have allowed a freer circulation of oxygen, preventing damp and prolonging the life of the timber floor.

In London, traces of plank floors were also found in several broadly contemporary sunken-floored structures, excavated on the Cannon Street and Bucklersbury sites (Grimes 1968, 157, 159). Better-preserved examples of planked floors supported on joists are known from sunken-floored structures of the late 10th and 11th centuries found at Coppergate, York (Hall 1982, 240) and at Wallingford, Oxon (Durham 1980, 44; Fig 15). The plank floor of the Coppergate building was cut carefully to fit flush around the bases of the vertical wall posts and, like the London Building WAT3, was supported on longitudinally-aligned joists (Hall 1984a, 71). However, timber impressions of the wall posts of the Wallingford building suggest that the joists supporting the floor were notched into them.

Entrances

Evidence of an entrance was found in two surface-laid buildings (PDN4, PDN5) and three sunken-floored structures (MLK1, PDN2, WEL7). In addition, the fragmentary remains of a wooden door were found in the demolition debris from Building PDN5.

The complete width of the doorway was preserved in only one example, Building MLK1. It was 1.6m wide, exactly double the distance between the individual wall posts. The doorways of Buildings PDN4 and PDN5 were at least 1.4m wide,

SLB = surface-laid building
pl = planks
ch = crushed chalk
b/e = beaten earth
s = sand

SFS = sunken-floored structure
org = rushes or grasses
mort = mortar
br/e = brickearth
gr = gravel

Building	CP	Type	pl	org	ch	mort	b/e	br/e	s	gr
PEN8	1	SLB							x	
PEN9	1	"					x			
PEN10	1	"					x	x		
PEN4	1	"					x	x		
PEN2	1	"						x		
FMO1	1	SFS					x		x	x
MLK1	1	"					x			
WEL1	1	"					x			
PEN12	2	SLB						x		
PEN5	2	"					x	x		
PEN3	2	"					x	x		
MLK4	2	"						x		
MLK5	2	"						x		
FMO2	2	SFS					x		x	x
PDN1	2	"	x				x			
MLK2	2	"					x			
IRO1	2	"		x				[illegible]		
PDN3	3	SLB						x		
IRO3	3	"					x			
PDN6	3	"					x			
PEN7	3	"					x			
WAT1	3	SFS					x			
FMO3	3	"					x	x		
PDN2	3	"					x			
WAT4	3	"					x			
PDN4	4	SLB			x	x		x	x	
PDN5	4	"				x			x	
PDN7	4	"				x	x			
PDN8	4	"				x				
WEL6	4	"						x		
PDN11	4	SFS		x				x		x
WAT2	4	"					x			
WAT3	4	"	x				x	x	x	
FMO4	4	"					x			
PDN10	5	SLB				x		x		x

80. Floor types.

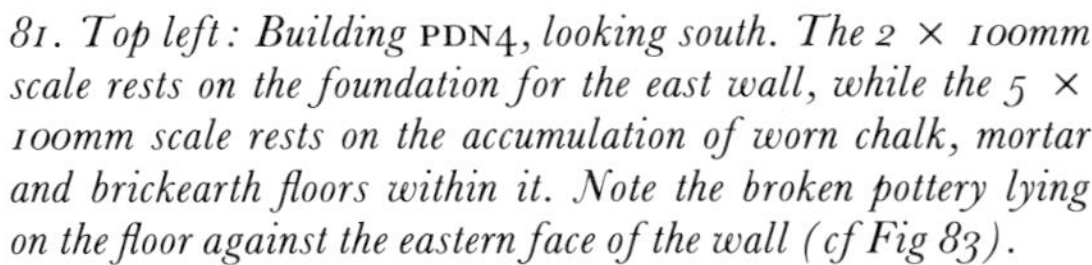

81. Top left: Building PDN4, *looking south. The 2 × 100mm scale rests on the foundation for the east wall, while the 5 × 100mm scale rests on the accumulation of worn chalk, mortar and brickearth floors within it. Note the broken pottery lying on the floor against the eastern face of the wall (cf Fig 83).*

82. Top right: Disturbed remains of the brickearth floor within sunken-floored Building PDN11, *looking south-east. The 2 × 100mm scale rests in an intrusion cut through the internal surface. Note the remains of a storage jar spread over the floor.*

83. Right: Building PDN4, *looking south. The 2 × 100mm scale rests on the foundation for the east wall, while the 5 × 100mm scale sits within the building in a worn area of the floor west of a thick accumulation of surfaces and occupation debris up against the wall (cf Fig 81).*

although their full width is unknown. Nevertheless, these entrances were almost twice as wide as the door, the fragmentary remains of which were recovered from the debris of the later Building PDN5 (see below). The doorways of contemporary buildings in Lincoln (Perring 1981, 7 Fig 6), Dublin (Murray 1983, 35), Chester (Mason 1985, Figs 8-10) and Rhuddlan (Blockley forthcoming) were slightly narrower, ranging from 1m to 1.27m in width.

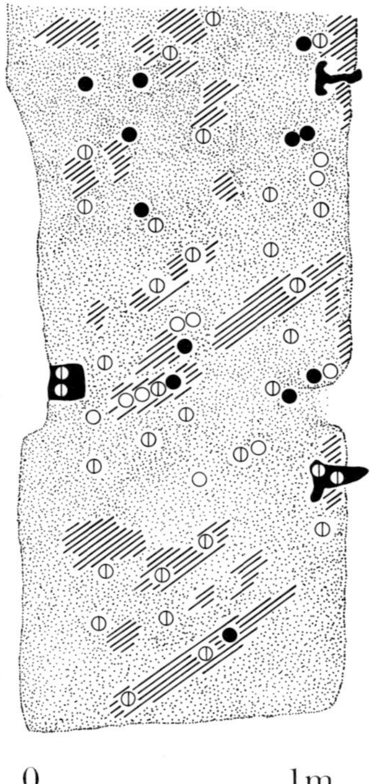

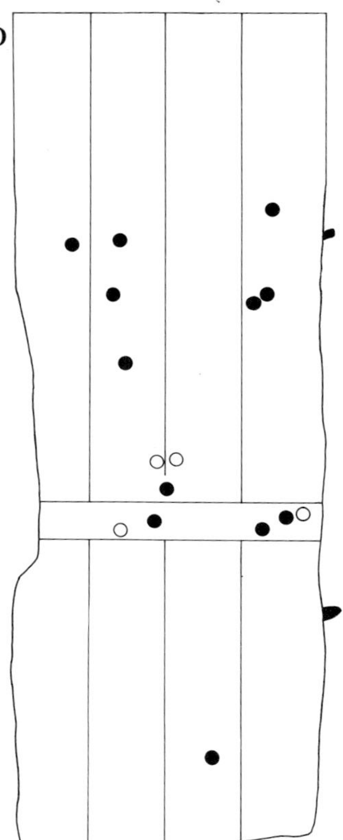

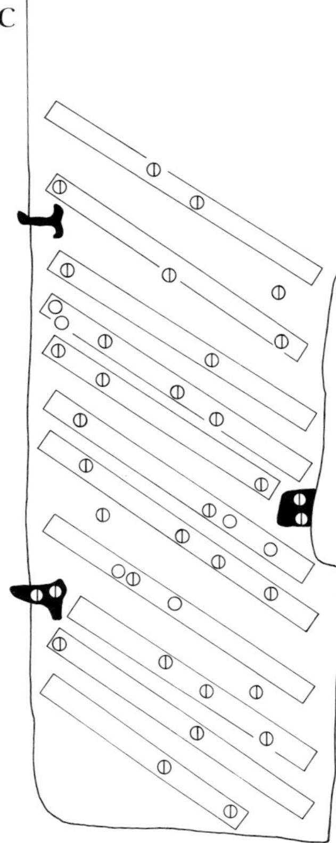

84. The Saxon door found on the Pudding Lane excavation: (cf Figs 11, 85 (PDN81)). a) The impression of the door, recorded on site as traces of wood-stain (shown hatched) around a scatter of nails. Nails with heads upwards are shown as black dots; nails with shanks uppermost as bisected circles. b) Suggested reconstruction of the external face of the door, showing vertical boards with a horizontal batten reinforcing the lock. c) Suggested reconstruction of the internal face, showing the position of hinges and diagonal battens.

Doorframe

The doorframe of the sunken-floored Building MLK1 had been dismantled and the timber removed in antiquity. Nevertheless, sufficient evidence remained to indicate it was built of circular earthfast posts, up to 0.2m across, set against the outer face of the wall, parallel to the wall-posts. The door-posts were set 0.21m and 90mm into the ground, the post with the greater depth indicating the side of the frame on which the door was hung.

Threshold bar

Evidence of a threshold bar was found in the sunken-floored Buildings MLK1 and WEL7. In the earlier structure (MLK1) it was formed by the lowest run of wall planking and in the later example (WEL7) by the baseplate supporting the east wall. Threshold bars in broadly contemporary structures excavated in Dublin were separate horizontal timbers dowelled to the inner or outer faces of the door jambs (Murray 1983, 66).

Steps

Two examples of earthen steps providing access to sunken-floored Buildings MLK1 WEL7 were found, but in only one instance (MLK1) did traces of a wooden staircase survive, perhaps similar to that suggested for the sunken-floored structures found in Chester (Mason 1985, 20). Traces of an

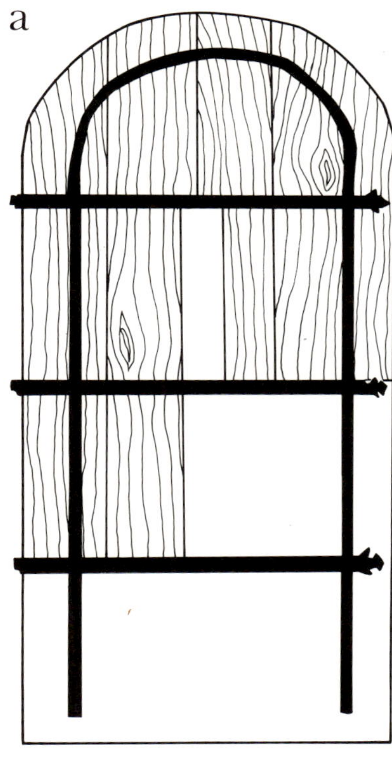

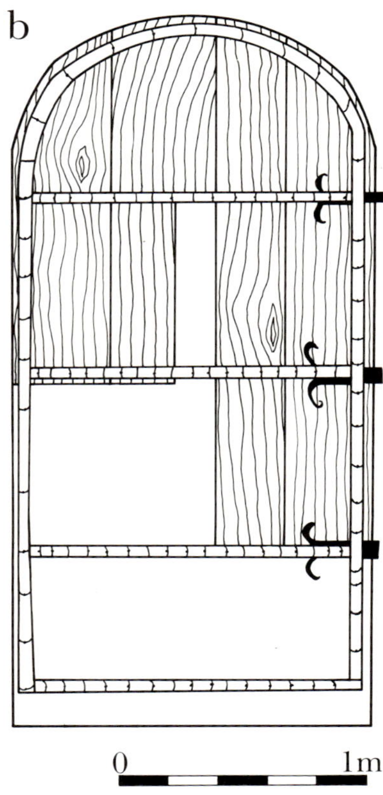

85. Door from St Botolph's Church, Hadstock (cf Fig 84). a) The external face, with the iron straps shown in black. b) The internal face, showing the hinges.

earthen stair were also found at the entrance to sunken-floored buildings in Ipswich (Dunmore et al. 1976, 135; Fig 47), and Oxford (Jope 1958, 13-4). By contrast, a compacted beaten-earth ramp with a gradual slope led down into sunken-floored Building PDN2. At Thetford, access to the cellar in Structure J was by way of a ramped passage of similar construction (Davison 1967, 192; Fig 52).

Porch

Evidence of a porch protecting the entrance was found in three examples (PDN4, PDN5, WEL7), one of which was sunken-floored. Although little trace of the porch of Building WEL7 survived, decayed woodstain marking the line of the north wall indicated that it was supported on a baseplate. No trace of the porch walls of Buildings PDN4 and PDN5 survived, but the preservation of accumulated brickearth, crushed chalk and sand floors laid across the wall foundation, extending at least 0.8m beyond the doorway indicate its extent. The better-preserved remains of a porch similar in type to Building WEL7 were found at the entrance to Hut Pit 2, a contemporary sunken-floored structure excavated near Cannon Street, London (Grimes 1968, 157). No evidence was found of stone-revetted sunken passages similar to those providing access to the sunken-floored structures recorded in York and Lincoln on sites at Coppergate (Hall 1984a, 74; Figs 4-5) and St Paul-in-the-Bail (Webster and Cherry 1980, 227-8).

Door

(Figs 84-6)

In the remains of the demolition debris of Building PDN5 the fragmentary remains of a door were found. After the deliberate demolition of the building, the door had been dragged from its original position in the porch on the west wall and dumped close to the east wall, where it survived as a pattern of ironwork in very decayed wood and woodstain. The ironwork, which consisted of

87. Building PEN6 *looking north-west. The 2 × 100mm scale rests on the internal brickearth floor to the south of a slot for a bench or similar feature.*

nails, hinges and a bolt, was extremely corroded and the only recognisable surviving wooden elements were the remains of eleven diagonal wooden battens. However, sufficient remained to allow an almost complete reconstruction.

The London door consisted of a single leaf, 2.3m × 0.8m × 50mm, formed from approximately four vertical oak boards *c.*35mm thick, secured on their internal faces by eleven diagonal battens 0.72m × 60mm × 15mm. Each of these was anchored to the boards by some four nails. The boards were further secured by a single horizontal wooden batten nailed across the external face of the door to protect the fastening. The sag in its outer or fastening edge suggests that this well-constructed London door was fairly old by the time it was dumped. Indeed it may even have been transferred from one or more of earlier buildings preceding PDN5, as they were replaced.

The door hinges were in the crescent style and very similar to those on the north door at St Botolph's Church, Hadstock, Essex, one of the very few surviving doors of this period (Geddes 1982). This door was recently re-examined and drawn by Christine Milne (with the kind permission of the Rector), and is shown in Fig 86. However, the Hadstock hinges extend across the external face of the door as substantial iron straps and the only hint of any hinge attachment on the front of the Pudding Lane door is provided by two nails aligned with the upper hinge. These may have secured a wooden strap but equally the random spread of nails on the outer face of the door may originally have held decorative ironwork similar to that still surviving on the door of the later church at Stillingfleet in Yorkshire (Addyman 1976).

*86. The 2 × 100mm scale rests on an external surface excavated on the Pudding Lane site. The rusted remains of iron nails and traces of wooden battens are all that remains of a discarded Saxon door (cf Fig 84) (*PDN81*).*

Windows

Three fragments of window glass were found within cellared Building WAT3, in two cases within layers indicative of use (see Finds Catalogue in *Volume II*, Vince forthcoming, Nos 192-4). One fragment (No 192) was found in an organic layer covering the floor area, incorporat-

Hearths

Type I = scorched floor
Type 2 = brickearth slab
Type 3 = timber-retained slab

Date	type I	type 2	type 3
CP I	MLK I	PEN9	
		*	
		MLK I	
		PEN I O	
CP2		PEN5	
		*	
		*	
		*	
		*	
		*	
CP3		PEN7	PEN7
		*	
		*	
		*	
		PEN I 3	

Ovens

Type I = brickearth & rubble slab
Type 2 = brickearth slab
Type 3 = basin in platform
Type 4 = basin in rubble base

Date	type I	type 2	type 3	type 4
CP I	PEN2			PEN2
	PEN4			*
	*			
CP2	WEL3	PEN3	PEN I I	IRO2
				PEN I 2
CP3		PEN7		
CP4				PDN5
				WEL6

* = each additional hearth of the same type.

88. Hearth and oven types: Ovens and hearths listed under the numbers of the buildings in which they were found.

89. The hearth in sunken-floored Building MLK I*, looking east. The 10 × 100mm scale rests on the internal surface beyond which is the entrance, disturbed by modern foundations.*

ing straw and wood. The excavator thought this layer may have been associated with the occupation of the building or may have been decayed timber or rush/straw floor. A series of timbers which may have been joists were laid over this and another organic layer recorded over that contained a second piece of glass (No 193). A later dumped deposit within the building thought to represent preparation for further building work contained the third fragment (No 194). In addition, two more fragments of glass (Nos 195-6) were found in the fill of a pit of the same Ceramic Phase, which lay next to and respected the line of the south wall of Building WAT2. The implication is that cellared Buildings WAT2 and WAT3 had glass windows somewhere in the superstructure.

90. Circular hearth within sunken-floored Building IRO2, *set into the floor on which the 10 × 100mm scale rests.*

91. The oven in the south-west corner of Building WEL3, *next to the 5 × 100mm scale. Note the postholes and stakeholes marking the building's south and west walls.*

a

b

92. The oven in Building WEL3, *with 2 × 100mm scale, showing: a) the tile and rubble base overlain by b) the brick-earth floor of the oven.*

93. (top) The oven in Building PEN3, *with the 2 × 100mm scale resting on the floor. Note the burnt wattle-work strengthening the brickearth walls.*

94. (bottom) The 10 × 10mm scale rests on the timber-framed base of the oven within Building PEN11 *(cf Fig 96).*

a

b

95. The oven in Building PEN12, *with 2 × 100mm scale, showing: a) rubble base b) collapsed brickearth superstructure: stakeholes mark the line of the circular oven wall.*

Partitions

Traces of internal partition walls were recorded in four surface-laid structures (PEN8, PDN4-6) employing different types of construction. Evidence of an *earthfast wattle* partition of this type was found in two structures (PEN8, PDN6). The posts were set at irregular intervals, but little trace of the interwoven wattle screens survived. All that remained of the partition subdividing the north extension of Building PDN5 was the impression of *planking set on edge*, but it is not known exactly what form the associated superstructure would have taken. The slightly better-preserved remains of a partition with *wattles set in a baseplate* were found in Building PDN4. The carbonized remains of the wattle screen were recorded, and the position of the baseplate was marked by the slot in which it had been laid. Partitions of this type are known from contemporary buildings excavated in Dublin (Murray 1983, 132) and York (Hall 1982, 240). In the absence of more detailed evidence, it is not possible to determine the original heights of the London partitions, although it is assumed that they rose at least to the top of the walls.

Internal Fittings

(Fig 87)

Slight traces of internal fixtures and fittings were found in numerous structures but in only two examples did detailed evidence survive. In the south-east corner of Building PDN3, remains of a timber-revetted bench were found, similar to the walls of contemporary buildings excavated in Dublin (Murray, 1983 37-8) and York (Hall brushwood and earth-packed benches lining the 1984, 53-55, Fig 52). The carbonized remains of a planked wooden bench were recorded against a section of the east wall of Building PDN4.

Hearths and ovens

(Fig 88)

The most common features found within the buildings were *hearths*, or open fireplaces, and *ovens*, enclosed receptacles for baking. The majority were centrally-positioned, that is to say, were set directly under the roof ridge. This pattern is shared by the hearths and ovens found in contemporary buildings in York (Hall 1984a, 53), Lincoln (Perring 1981, 39), Thetford (Davison 1971, 37), and Dublin (Murray 1983, 9). In London, exceptions to this general rule were the oven set in the south-west corner of Building WEL3 and the hearth in the northern extension of Building PDN5. In total, the remains of 28 hearths and ovens were recorded, the evidence for which is shown in Fig 88.

Hearths

(Figs 89, 90)

Three types of hearth were identified, ranging from a scorched area of the floor surface, to a brickearth slab, to a brickearth slab contained within a timber revetment. Evidence of only one hearth of the *scorched floor* type was found, in sunken-floored Building MLK1. Ash and charcoal deposits over the scorched area suggest it was the site of an open wood fire, probably used for domestic purposes. Hearths of this type were common in 11th-century buildings found in Dublin (Murray 1983, 130, 139, 155).

Far more common in London was the *brickearth slab* hearth, of which 14 examples have been found (PEN9, PEN10, PEN5, PEN3, PEN7, PEN13, MLK1) in structures of 9th- to 11th-century date (CP1-3). These slabs were usually 40mm thick, very compacted and irregular in shape. All were scorched. Stakeholes around three of these hearths provided evidence of supports for cooking utensils. There was no evidence to suggest that these were other than domestic fireplaces. Hearths of similar construction are known from York in the 10th century (Addyman 1980, 38), and were found in 10th- to 12th-century structures at Lincoln (Perring 1981, 6-33). A hearth found in the annexe to the 11th-century Building L at Thetford may be of the same type (Davison 1967, 192; Fig 51: Carolyn Dallas, pers comm).

Structures thought to represent hearths comprising *brickearth slabs set within a timber revetment* were found in Buildings PEN5 and PEN7. The compacted brickearth slab was 5-20mm thick, but unfortunately only the impressions of the timberwork survived. Hearths contained within similar timber or stone revetments are known from York (Addyman 1980, 38) and Dublin. Associated with a 10th-century example from York were many fragments of crucibles and other containers for molten metal, which suggests that it was used for metalworking (Hall 1984, 53, 55-6). By contrast, the 11th-century Dublin examples appear to have been used purely for domestic purposes (Murray 1983, 96).

Ovens

(Figs 91-6)

Several types of oven were found: some were built at ground-level, others were set into the floor, and some incorporated platforms or rubble bases. The remains of three ovens built at ground level over a *brickearth and rubble slab* were found in Buildings PEN2, PEN4, WEL3, dated to the late 9th to 11th century (CP1 and 2). The oven bases were built of fragments of re-used Roman tile, flint and limestone set in, or capped by, slabs of brickearth, while the rubble base of one (WEL3) was set on gravel. The surface of the brickearth in all examples was scorched. The evidence of the superstructure was only well-preserved in one of the later examples (WEL3). Here, the brickearth walls had originally been supported by a framework of 33 angled stakes. The outline of this superstructure was reflected by the blackened surface of the brickearth, scorched in an arc around the stone-filled heat-reservoir, noted above. Fragments of quern stone and samples of carbonized grain were recovered from this oven, which led to the suggestion that it may have also been used for drying grain. Evidence of features with a similar base was found in a rural context at the Anglo-Saxon village of West Stow, where two examples also yielded samples of carbonised grain (West 1969, 11).

96. Plan of a timber-framed oven base in Building PEN11. *Burnt areas are shaded; brickearth is shown hatched and gravel stippled (cf Fig 94).*

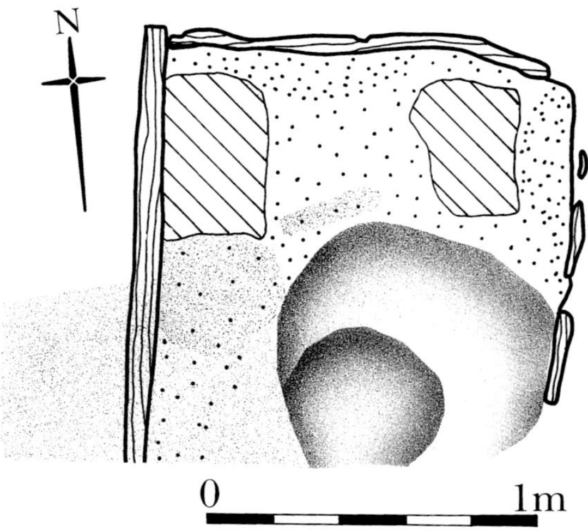

Building no.	date	length	width	depth
PEN2	CP1	0.4m	0.3m	0.4m
*	CP1	?	?	?
PEN12	CP2	0.9m in diameter		0.6m
IRO2	CP2	*c*.2m	*c*.1.5m	0.09
PDN5	CP4	0.52m	0.48m	0.26m
WEL6	CP4	?	?	0.3m

* = additional oven within the same building

97. The dimensions of oven basins set into rubble bases.

Broadly contemporary structures with a similar base are known from Durham (Carver 1979, 16), Dublin (Murray 1983, 37; Fig 38), Lincoln (Perring 1981, 6-33) and York (Hall 1984a, Fig 155). The Lincoln structures were interpreted as hearths and scatters of stakeholes around them were assumed to mark the site of vertically-set stakes supporting windbreaks or cooking utensils (Perring 1981, 42). However, these stakes may well have supported an oven superstructure. Conversely, the absence of superstructural evidence may indicate that the York and Dublin structures, although virtually identical in construction to the London oven bases, were in fact hearths.

Two examples of an oven base comprising a *brickearth slab* were found (PEN3, PEN7). The brickearth slab, up to 30mm thick, was compacted with a scorched surface. The remains of two burnt brickearth wall stubs, 200mm wide, survived up to 300mm high in one instance (PEN3), where the walls were raised over a footing of tile fragments. The brickearth wall stubs around the other example (PEN7) show that it too was originally roofed.

Other types of oven incorporated *basins set into platforms* of gravel or rubble. One oven (PEN11) had been set into a gravel platform *c*.2.2m × 1.4m and 50mm high, built of well-compacted sand and gravel, capped with brickearth. It was retained by a framework of four planks, *c*.5mm thick, laid flat. The timberwork was heavily decayed but the north-east corner was sufficiently well-preserved to show that the planks formed a simple butt joint. At least two timbers, those planks retaining the northern and western sides of the platform, had squared ends. The oven basin was sunk into the presumed centre of the platform. It was circular, 0.40m in diameter by 50mm deep, lined with a compacted slab of brickearth. Its mouth was apparently on the west side. This type of construction would have served to protect the hearth from rising damp which, with frequent re-heating, could have caused the brickearth to disintegrate (Bowler 1985; PEN79 Archive Report, TS 754). The brickearth lining, although well-fired, showed no sign of the extremely high temperatures that might be expected in an industrial furnace and was most probably used in baking. No exact parallels for this type of oven construction are known.

The remains of six ovens with *basins set into rubble bases* were found (PEN2, IRO2, PEN12, PDN5, WEL6) although evidence of the superstructure was preserved in only two instances. The basins varied in size and shape and were lined with gravel or brickearth. Three examples (PDN5, PEN2, PEN12) incorporated a rubble base mostly built of fragments of reused Roman tile. Traces of brickearth walls supporting the superstructure were recorded in two examples (WEL6, PEN2), and the walls of the latter had been strengthened with wattle. This hearth had a flue and was found to contain significant quantities of carbonized grain which could suggest that it may have been used used for drying grain. Ovens of similar construction are known from Lincoln, ranging in date from 970 to 1200 (Perring 1981, 6-33), and at least two of these examples had been used for glass-working (Perring 1981, 42 Nos F8, F9).

7: RECONSTRUCTING THE BUILDINGS

Valerie Horsman

Introduction

The remains of several of the London buildings were sufficiently well-preserved to allow reconstruction on paper, and in this section an attempt is made to reconstruct one sunken-floored structure (PDN2) and one surface-laid building (PDN3). The exercise combined the careful study of the archaeological evidence with the subsequent appraisal of better-preserved remains of similar buildings found on other sites in London, York and Dublin.

The sunken-floored building PDN2

(Fig 98: see Catalogue, p.38)

Although much of this building had been destroyed by Victorian foundations, sufficient evidence remained to indicate that it was rectangular, *c*.5.5m long by 3.7m wide, set in a sub-rectangular construction pit 0.41m deep (Fig 24). Access to the sunken-floor level was by way of a gradually sloping ramp at the north end of the building. All that remained of the walls was a section of collapsed earth bank and levelled padstones laid around the base of the construction pit, on which a timber base-plate would have been supported. Immediately inside and parallel to the line of padstones, were several deeply-driven stakes which would have secured the base of a timber framework retaining the earth bank. These stakes had stood at least 100mm above the internal surface, and their height and spacing presumably reflects the thickness and the lengths of the individual pieces of timber comprising the baseplates.

It is possible to show that the earth bank had actually been built with upcast from the excavation of the construction pit. After the demolition of the building, the earth bank was used to infill the sunken area. Significantly, large articulated lumps of characteristically-laminated waterlaid deposit were preserved within this infill. It was into just such deposits that the foundation pit had originally been dug, and hence it is argued that the initial upcast was utilised more or less in situ, and with minimum disturbance, as the earth walling for the building.

The height of the collapsed earth wall, added to the depth of the construction pit, suggests that the walls of Building PDN2 could have stood up to *c*.1.5m high. However, allowing for some dispersal of the bank as it collapsed, it is suggested that the wall was initially just over 1m in height. The volume of earth excavated from the site of Building PDN2 was *c*.8.35 cubic metres, which would certainly have provided sufficient material for a wall of that size. The bank must have been scarped since no evidence of an external wooden revetment was found. Thus the bank would have been just over 1m wide at its base, approximately the same width as the walls of turf houses excavated at Hound Tor and Hutholes in Devon (Beresford 1979, 114). The inner face of the bank would have been retained by timberwork, but the batter on the outer face would not have discouraged the growth of grass, which was probably deliberately cultivated to contain erosion.

The remains of another broadly contemporary timber-retained earth-walled building were recorded on the Cannon Street site (Grimes 1968, 155-7). This structure, known as Hut Pit 1, was 3.5m long by 2.74m wide and set at least 0.9m into the ground (Grimes 1968, Figs 34-5). Although badly disturbed by later activity, traces of the earth bank were preserved on its east side. It had been prevented from collapsing into the construction pit by a timber framework built of wooden planks secured by large earthfast posts. These posts were set in D-shaped postholes and may have been tree trunks split in half.

Better-preserved buildings employing a similar type of post-and-plank construction have been excavated at Coppergate in York, providing invaluable detail for the present reconstruction

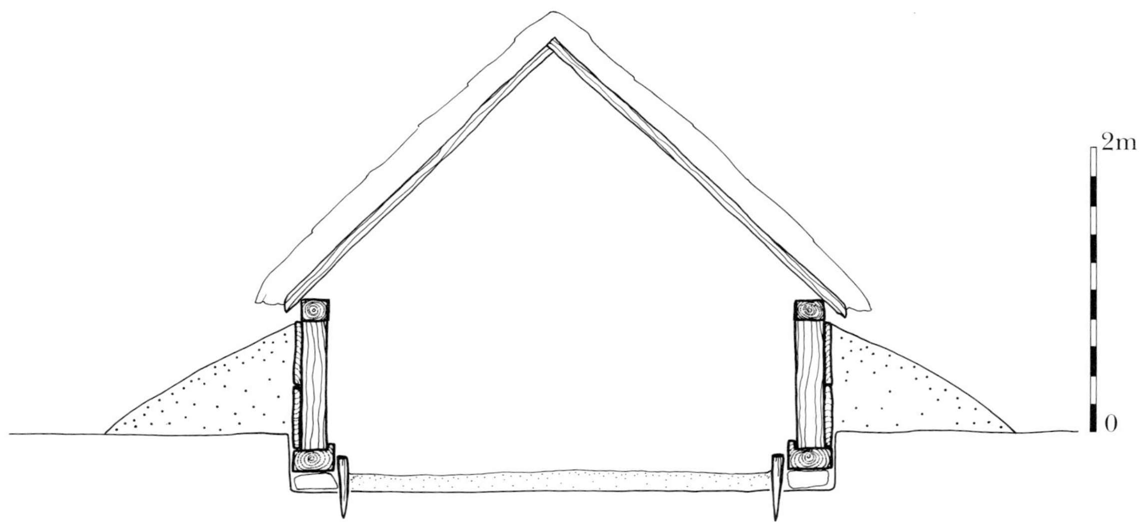

98. Reconstructed west-east section through sunken-floored Building PDN2 *with earth banks retained by post and plank walls (cf Fig 99).*

(Hall 1982, 238-40). In contrast to the London building (PDN2), the York buildings were set very deeply into the ground, on average penetrating *c.*1.5m below the surface. They were built of planks laid edge-to-edge, retained against the side of the construction pit by rectangular posts (Fig 99). These posts were either supported on baseplates laid in gullies around the bottom of the construction pit or were set in shallow trenches often resting on small wooden pads. In those examples in which a baseplate was used, the lowest course of planking rested on its upper surface. To prevent the upright posts slipping under pressure of the earth, the baseplates had an inner shoulder.

The London Building PDN2 presumably employed a similar type of retaining framework for the inner face of the earth bank. It would probably have incorporated planking fixed to posts set vertically into base-plates laid over the levelled padstones. Baseplates similar to those used in York have been recorded in London and therefore baseplates of this type are shown in the reconstruction. The baseplates were secured by deeply-driven stakes set at intervals along the wall. Tie-beams would have been necessary to prevent inward movement of the upper part of the timber retaining walls under pressure from the earth bank. These beams could have been set into wall plates or perhaps they could have articulated directly with the heads of paired posts. Given that no trace of independent roof supports was found and that the *c.*1m wide earth-bank was scarped, it is possible (though not certain) that the entire weight of the roof was carried by the timber revetment. Thus, corner posts would have been necessary to ensure the rigidity of the timber framework. Since their position was not marked by postholes, these timbers must have been housed in the baseplates.

There was no direct evidence regarding the roofing material employed. A thatch roof is illustrated in the reconstruction drawing, although other possibilities, such as turf, should be considered. The optimum angle for drainage of a thatched roof is approximately 45°. With a roof pitch at this angle and a wall height of 1.2m, the roof would have been 3.10m tall in the centre.

The greater part of this building would have protruded well above ground level but the outer earthen face, probably grassed over, would have hidden the timber walls. Thus the doorway, which was probably about 0.8m wide would have probably provided the only source of natural light. In this respect, Building PDN2 was similar to other single-storied post-and-plank buildings sunk much deeper into the ground, of which examples are known from elsewhere in London (see Fig 106) and the country. Other parallels for this type of earth-walled building have been recorded in Scandinavia and also in Iceland where examples of 11th-century turf buildings of similar appearance have recently been excavated (Graham-Campbell and Kidd 1980, 78, pl 33).

99. Coppergate excavations, York. Construction detail from a 10th-century timber building, showing lipped-baseplate (on which 2 × 100mm scale sits) retaining the foot of a vertical post with plank cladding behind. (Photo by Mike S Duffy, published by permission of the York Archaeological Trust).

The surface-laid building PDN3

(Fig 100: see Catalogue, p.39)

Much of Building PDN3 had also been destroyed by Victorian concrete foundations but sufficient evidence survived to show that it was rectangular, *c.*6.4m long by *c.*3.2m wide. It was terraced into the slope of the hillside, the ground level outside the building being 0.5m higher than the internal floor at the northern end. All that remained of the walls were timber impressions up to 150mm deep and lines of decayed wood stain up to 0.24m wide, representing the wooden baseplates which once supported the superstructure. For the western and most of the eastern wall, the baseplates rested on a line of carefully-levelled stones set in a shallow trench (Fig 101). By contrast, the southern end of the eastern baseplate was levelled on timber chocks and wedges (Fig 102) while the southern baseplate was laid directly onto the ground surface. Access to the building is assumed to have been at the southern end, at which point the internal and external surface levels were the same.

Examination of the better preserved sections of woodstain from the walls showed that they represented timbers which had been allowed to decay *in situ*, thus revealing details of the building's construction. For example, it was clear that the eastern baseplate had been butted up against the southern one, even though the south-east corner of the building had been slightly displaced as a result of subsidence or later disturbance. Even more significant was the recovery of evidence for a longitudinal groove cut into the upper face of the baseplate, represented by a band of silt running the length of the baseplate with impressions of timber on both sides (Fig 103).

A close parallel was found in Dublin on the Christchurch Place excavations (Murray 1983, 95, Fig 138). This building was also laid out over the remains of earlier buildings, but, in contrast to the London building, was largely undisturbed by later intrusions, and much of the timberwork survived in excellent condition in situ (Fig 104). This structure was *c.*8m long by *c.* 4.85m wide and incorporated wooden baseplates laid on a levelled foundation of stones, rough branches and other

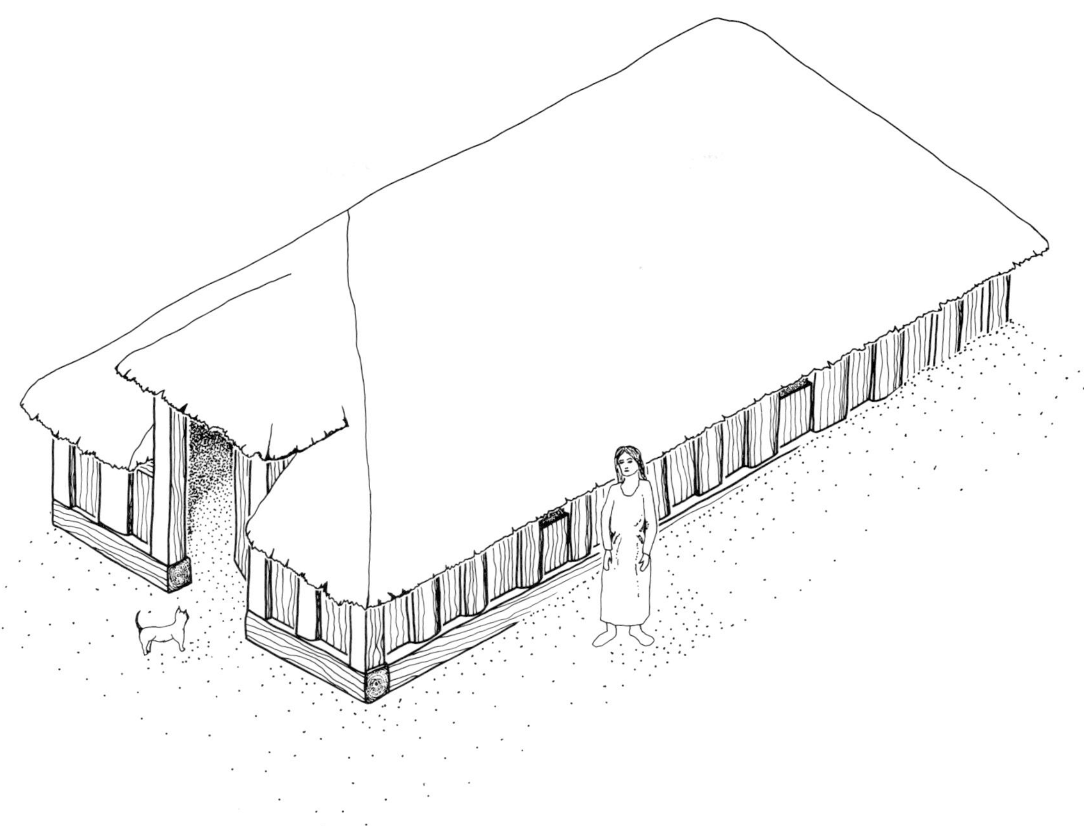

100. Isometric reconstruction of London Building PDN3, *showing the low walls and a hipped roof. (After Richard Lea in Horsman 1985).*

timbers. These baseplates, although broken in several places, had originally been cut from a single length of timber, and were joined at the corners by half-lap joints. They were similar in width to those from the London building and also had a central groove, in which, however, the bases of vertical planks and staves were also found (Fig 105). These were best preserved along the east wall of the building where they comprised an arrangement of alternately-set staves with a convex outer face, a flat inner face and grooves up both edges, together with thinner flat planks tapered up both sides to fit these grooves. A junction of the walls was preserved in the south-east corner where the end of the plank in the baseplate forming the lower member of the half-lap joint lay across the end of the upper baseplate abutting its end plank at right angles, without a corner post.

A timber recovered from inside the Dublin building was thought to be a displaced stave from the east wall. At its base, it was similar to the staves in situ in the wall but, 1m above its base, its sides were tapered like those of the thin planks suggesting that all the wall members were tapered at the top to fit a wall plate. Such a wall-plate would have been necessary to hold the wall cladding together and would have been simple to construct since the walls of the building were straight and its corners right-angled.

A group of four earthfast posts in the interior of the building represented support for the roof, implying that the walls were not strong enough to carry such a weight unaided. Although there was no trace of the door jambs, a passage with plank flooring flanked by vertical planks set in a grooved baseplate clearly indicated the position of the entrance to the building. It was off-centre on one of its long walls, unlike that in the London building.

Since both buildings had similar, carefully-prepared levelled footings and grooved baseplates, it is suggested that the London building may have had stave and plank walls similar to those in Dublin. Thus the reconstruction drawing (Fig 100) shows the outer face of the east and south walls of the London building with convex staves and thinner flat planks set alternately into a baseplate. The planks would have been tapered up both sides to slot into grooves up the edges of the staves, and all the wall members would have been tapered at the top to fit a wall-plate. Similar timbers with grooves along both edges and a tapered end were found during the excavations on the nearby Billingsgate Lorry Park site, where they had been reused in an early 13th-century

101. East wall of Building PDN3, *looking south-west. The 5 × 100mm scale sits on the internal floor which is bounded along its eastern edge by the levelled stone foundation upon which the timber-framed east wall rested. Note the Nierdermendig lava quern stone reused in the foundation to the south of the 2 × 100mm scale.*

102. South-east corner of Building PDN3, *looking west. The 2 × 100mm scale rests on the internal floor. The impression of the baseplate and of wedges driven beneath it can clearly be seen on the line of the east wall.*

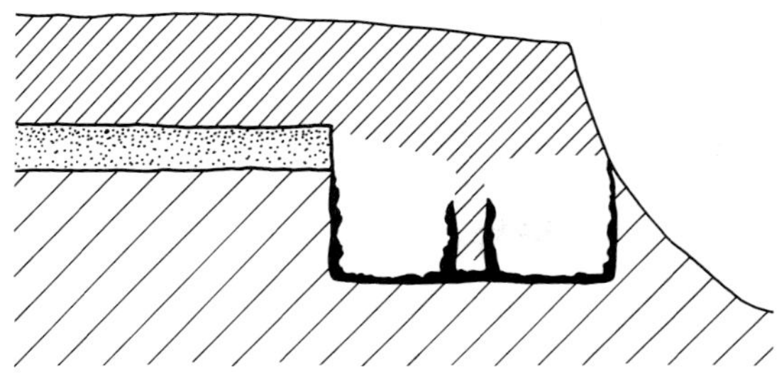

103. Schematic section through the footings of the east wall of Building PDN3. *Grey silts (shown here with closely-spaced hatching) sealed the internal floor (shown stippled) and the wall foundation, preserving the impression of a grooved baseplate.*

revetment. They had presumably been derived from earlier, dismantled buildings in the waterfront area.

The stave walls of the London building may have abutted each other at right angles without corner posts, just like the Dublin walls. However, as there is no evidence that the London roof was supported on independent roof posts such as those found in the larger Dublin building, it must be assumed that its weight was carried solely by the walls. It is therefore far more likely that the wall planks fitted into grooved corner posts which would have provided more stability. Since no trace of any earthfast corner posts was found in the surviving south-east corner of the building, it is assumed that the corner posts were set in the baseplates. Similar grooved corner posts were in fact recovered from an earlier well to the west of the building in 1981 (Fig 77), suggesting that the occupants of the property were familiar with that building technique.

The size of these walls cannot be precisely established, but need not have been carried to head height, as recent work has shown. A complete but displaced wall plank from the east wall of the Dublin building tapered 1m above its base, which implies that its walls cannot have stood much above 1.2m. In addition, a complete but collapsed wattle wall of that height was excavated in Dublin, on the nearby Fishamble Street site. The advantage of such low walls lies principally in their more sparing use of timber. Although standing room would have been limited to the central area of these buildings, the space against its walls could have been used effectively for beds or benches. Given the close structural similarities between the London and Dublin buildings described here, it is suggested that the London building may also have incorporated low walls. The height of the walls shown in Fig 100 is therefore estimated at *c.*1.2m, on the basis of the Dublin examples.

It is assumed that the entrance to the building was at its southern end where the internal and external surfaces were at the same level. The height and width of this doorway are estimated respectively at 1.75m and 0.8m. These measurements are based on the average height of contemporary humans, deduced from the evidence collected from Saxon cemetery excavations, and from the width of the late Saxon door found discarded in the debris of a later building found on the Pudding Lane site (see pp.37-50 above and Horsman 1983, 31). The door jambs were probably mounted on the baseplates for the southern wall, since their position was not marked by postholes. The similarity of the levels of the contemporary internal and external surfaces at this point implies that the baseplate did not extend across the threshold as a threshold bar.

It is not possible to determine from the excavated evidence whether the roof was gable-ended or hipped. However the construction of the low walls, presumably favoured for their sparing use of timber, suggests that the roof could have been hipped for the same reason. The dimensions of the hip shown in the reconstruction are based upon the width of a bay in the building which

105. Christchurch Place excavations, Dublin. Isometric reconstruction of stave and plank wall from Building CP85/1 *(cf Fig 104).*

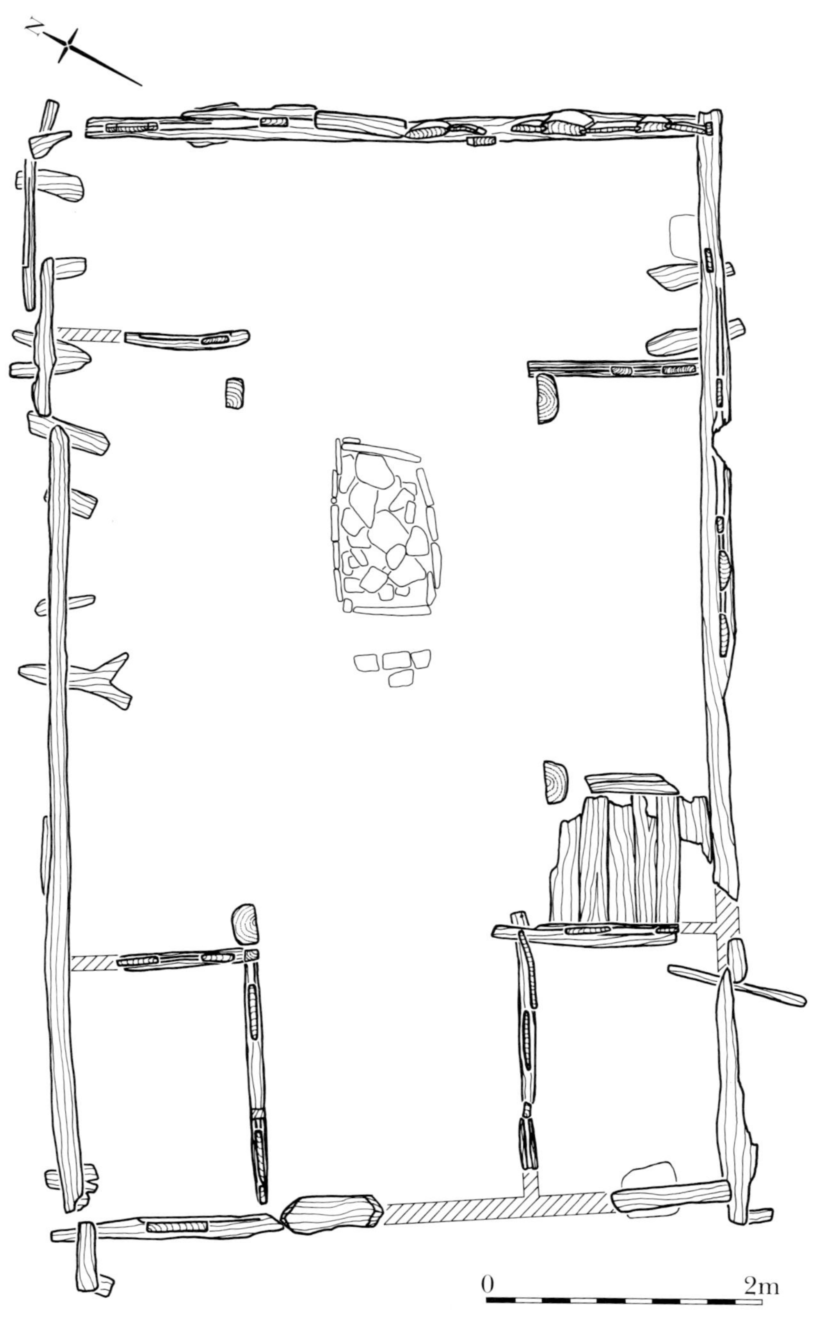

104. Christchurch Place excavations, Dublin. Plan of pre-Conquest Building CP85/1, *showing the well-preserved baseplates laid over a foundation of wood and stone: note the survival of a stave wall in the east. The conjectured wall is shown hatched. Unlike the London Building* PDN3, *the roof of this structure was supported by free-standing posts. (After Murray 1983, Fig 38: cf Fig 105).*

directly succeeded Building PDN3. In the absence of evidence to the contrary, it is assumed that the roof was thatched. If the roof was hipped, the doorframe on the southern gable wall would have protruded above the eaves. Whilst the door lintel would no doubt have been covered in thatch, the space between the jambs and the roof slope would probably have been boarded with vertical planks rising from a short baseplate similar to that excavated in the entrance passage of the Dublin building.

These tentative reconstructions present an interpretation of the appearance of just two of London's Saxon buildings. Obviously, it is difficult to evaluate the accuracy of this exercise, but two points need to be stressed. The first is that, whatever the preferred form of the reconstruction, the types of building represented differ markedly from the later timber-framed medieval buildings shown in the earliest surviving drawings and paintings of London. Different techniques and traditions are clearly in evidence. The second point is that there are far more types of buildings represented than are reconstructed in this report. Some techniques were certainly common, but none was universal: the buildings of Saxon London would have been notable more for their diversity than for their similarity.

8: DISCUSSION AND CONCLUSIONS

Valerie Horsman, Christine Milne and Gustav Milne

Building types

(Fig 106)

In the seven excavations considered in this report, two principal types of timber building were represented, surface-laid and sunken-floored buildings (see Part 4). Having established the different forms, an attempt was made to determine what differing uses these structures may have had. The assessment of their function considered various type of evidence, ranging from the associated finds and structural attributes to the position of the building in relation to the street system. Unfortunately, the artefactual material from the buildings and associated pits and wells was not especially informative with regard to establishing the specific function of particular buildings. However, it did provide important evidence of a more general nature, such as the bones of a pine-marten representing the presence of fur-traders and the group of quernstones reused in a foundation indicative of trade links with Germany, and these matters are discussed in detail in *Volume II.*

The ubiquitous surface-laid buildings with their hearths and ovens were evidently standard domestic dwellings. All the earliest examples of these buildings occupied sites which directly abutted the streets (WEL2, 3; PEN2, 4, 8, 9, 10), but in the later period (CP3) structures of this type were also erected at some distance from the main street frontage in areas previously occupied by outhouses or pits. For example, Building PDN3 was built over the site of an earlier sunken-floored structure (PDN2) in apparently open ground almost halfway between Botolph Lane and Fish Street Hill, and a similar pattern was recorded to the north of Cheapside, where Building IRO3 was laid out over the site of earlier sunken-floored structures. The construction of domestic dwellings on such previously under-developed sites suggests a significantly greater population density by the mid-11th century.

Some of the single-storied sunken-floored structures are interpreted as outhouses set behind the principal frontage in the back yard area. As such they could have performed, and presumably did, the variety of functions suggested for these buildings elsewhere (Rahtz 1976, 76, 81), ranging from workshops, stores or housing animals to temporary accommodation. However, the larger, better-built sunken-floored buildings, such as Building PDN11 and MLK1, seem to have been designed for permanent occupation.

106. Types of Saxon timber buildings found in London, shown in cross-section: a) surface laid building; b) outhouse with sunken floor; c) building with sunken floor; d) building with cellar below hall.

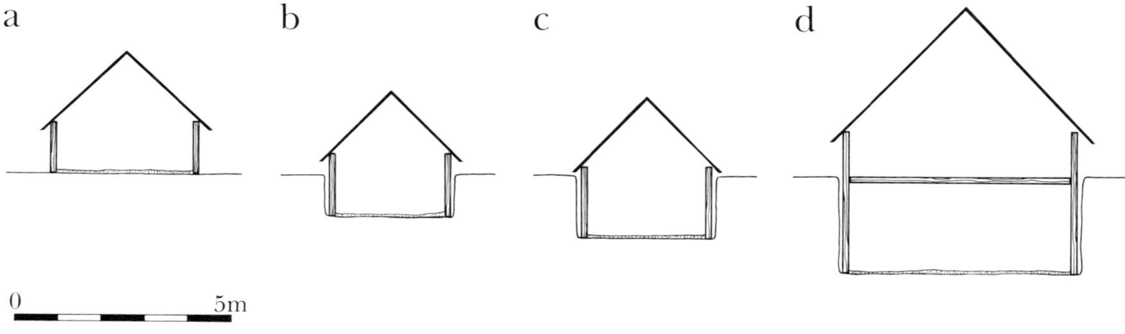

The more deeply-set sunken-floored buildings were part of ground-level structures beneath which, it is argued, the dark, window-less and hearth-less basement was used specifically for storage. The capacity of such basements seems larger than would be required for standard domestic needs, and implies that substantial quantities of particular commodities were stored for sale, or as part of a manufacturing process, or both. The presence of this specialised type of storage building is therefore seen as indicative of a commercial quarter in a settlement, and thus must be regarded as a specifically urban building type. Differences in construction technique may reflect the different types of material being stored. For example, attempts at providing especially water-proof walling in two buildings (WAT2, 3) may be contrasted with less elaborate techniques recorded on other buildings of this general type. Storage below ground, even in a timber building, would be less susceptible both to fire damage, the scourge of medieval towns, and to house-breaking.

The cellared buildings, like the outhouses, were built on land behind surface-laid buildings occupying the principal street frontages. The cellared buildings are not common before the 11th century (CP3 and 4), although two earlier examples were recorded to the east of Fish Street Hill (FMO1, 2), significantly close to the harbour near Billingsgate and to the principal north-south street leading to the market at Cheapside. However, the increase in buildings of this type in the half-century or so before the Norman Conquest implies that there was an increased need for storage facilities during that period, presumably reflecting a growth in commercial activity in the town. It is therefore suggested that, although many of the surface-laid buildings simply represent domestic dwellings, where they can be associated with the larger storage buildings, they may also be interpreted as the shops of merchants or craftsmen. Regrettably, only negative evidence was recovered for such surface-laid buildings directly associated with the cellared structures, in the form of unpitted areas up against the street frontage.

Although no Domesday Book returns survive for the City itself, indirect references to buildings in late Saxon London can be found elsewhere in that text. For example, in the returns for Surrey, properties in the City are sometimes assessed with properties in Southwark on the opposite bank of the Thames. Of the 111 holdings in London which are mentioned, about 50% are valued at between 2 and 7 pence (the smallest size); 35% at between 10 and 13 pence (up to twice the size) and 15% at 22 pence. Only one property was valued at a higher sum, 40 pence (Morris 1975). If these figures represent a valid sample, they would suggest a distinct social hierarchy in 11th-century London, a factor which would have manifested itself in further differences in the form and fabric of the buildings.

The longevity of the timber buildings

In order to establish the longevity of these early medieval buildings, the precise date of construction and destruction phases must be known. Unfortunately, such precision is not always attainable at present for Saxon features, for reasons outlined in Part 1. Nevertheless, wherever a substantial sequence of Saxon surfaces and structures was encountered, an assessment of the timespan represented has been attempted, from which a provisional statement on the longevity of the buildings can be made. For example, the series of 13 buildings adjacent to Botolph Lane (PEN1-13) represents continuous occupation of the area (although not necessarily of individual plots) over a period covering CP1-3, currently estimated as late 9th to the mid-11th century, some 150 to 200 years. During this period, the internal beaten-earth and brickearth floors underwent major resurfacing some 30 times, implying that internal floors were being renewed at intervals of five to ten years at most. The longest-lived building (PEN10) therefore probably stood for at least 40 years, although the majority of the others lasted for a minimum of between five and 25 years.

It should be stressed that these relatively modest lifespans are primarily a consequence of the frequency of fires in the town, of which several are listed in the *Anglo-Saxon Chronicle*. Even in the late 12th century, the frequency of fires was still considered a major drawback of living in London, according to William Fitzstephen. Such events were therefore a feared but accepted hazard of early medieval town life, in an era of open hearths, thatched roofs and wooden walls. Precisely because major fires were always anticipated, there seemed little point in over-elaborate construction or furnishing. A similar attitude to vernacular housing used to be prevalent in any area where natural disasters were irregular but common visitors, as in the hurricane belt for example. In London, more lavish constructions and richer furnishings only appear after the adoption of stricter building regulations, the wider use of masonry buildings, and the introduction of enclosed fireplaces in timber-framed buildings.

The temporary nature of Saxo-Norman buildings in London was therefore a reflection of the contemporary fear of fire, and need not be seen as a direct comment on the structural abilities of the house-builders. Indeed, it is argued that a building with a substantially longer life has been identified in the sequence excavated on the western side of Pudding Lane (Buildings PDN3-5). This area may well have been more or less open ground, and therefore the building which occupied it may have been less exposed to fire from neighbouring properties. The structural sequence incorporated several phases of internal surfaces usually of a more hard-wearing nature than those noted in other buildings. The period of activity represented extended from CP3 through CP4, a period extending from *c.*1000 to *c.*1125. An assessment of this site suggests that the eight major superimposed floors recorded there represent a life of at least 80 to 100 years for that particular much-modified building (Horsman 1985a, Archive Report PDN81 A, 14.27). This is comparable with the evidence from the Flaxengate site at Lincoln (Perring 1981), in which it is argued that major resurfacing of internal floors took place at 10 to 20 year intervals.

Building techniques

The evidence from the seven sites discussed in this report shows that the vernacular timber buildings of Saxo-Norman London were not all of the same type, since sunken-floored outhouses, single-storied surface-laid buildings and cellared buildings were all represented. Differing building techniques and traditions were also evident, with the recording of walls utilising earth-fast posts, staves, wattlework or baseplates. Such a variety of building techniques suggests that London did not have a building tradition peculiar to itself, but continuously adopted and adapted methods and styles from elsewhere. This is most certainly the pattern observed in the series of timber structures recently recorded from the excavation of the many 11th to 15th-century waterfront structures in the City (Milne 1985b). This implies that the builders had differing origins, and therefore brought to London new ideas and innovative approaches which were subsequently developed there. The series of modifications to the foundations of Buildings PDN3 to 5 present a telling example of such innovations which, it is argued, are characteristic of medieval London.

The topography of Saxo-Norman London

The study of the planned Saxon town, that is to say one which incorporates a grid of primary streets not of Roman origin, received considerable impetus following the excavations at Winchester in the 1960s and early 1970s, and particularly after the publication of an important article on the subject in 1971 (Biddle and Hill 1971). For London, it was noted that rectilinear street grids appear over two-thirds of the City on the earliest surviving maps. The general layout shown on those 16th-century plans is in essence little different from that shown on the first large-scale detailed survey of 1676/7, while documentary evidence implies that this pattern was certainly established by the 13th century.

What is in question is when and how the street system developed before that date. There is a certain though not slavish regularity reflected in the street system, but how much of that can be attributed to conscious planning in advance of road building? Did the street system develop from a series of primary streets such as Cheapside and Eastcheap to which other streets were gradually added, as some have implied (Brooke and Keir 1975, 171-2), or were whole grids laid out at once as others (eg Tatton-Brown 1986) have argued? If the latter was the case, which grid was established first, and how long a period elapsed before the next one was laid out? Does the pattern owe more to Saxon than to Norman Londoners, as Biddle and Hill suggested (Biddle and Hill 1971, 84) or was it simply the product of continuous accretion? The recent research on the development of Saxon properties and streets in the two study areas provides new data which will ultimately help to answer some of these questions.

The intra-mural area in the late Roman to late Saxon periods

With the notable exception of the town walls and associated gates, it is now clear that the underlying Roman urban topography exercised little influence on the form of the medieval street system. This is because the intra-mural area was cleared of most upstanding Roman buildings before the major late Saxon re-occupation of the area began, as recent archaeological work has shown. Indeed, Roman roads were exposed on three of the sites considered in this report, but not one directly influenced the form the medieval street plan subsequently took. It seems that the 9th-10th century City settlement was developed over fields rather than directly upon the crumbling ruins of a Roman town. This, at least, is a current interpretation of the standard sequence found on so many City sites, in which the Roman urban levels lie beneath an horizon of dark grey ploughsoil-like silt, which is in turn cut or sealed by late Saxon material.

These dark grey silt deposits have been the subject of some study and considerable debate. It is now clear that the deposits, which contain pottery and other artefacts, were the product of both dumping and accumulation, and depths of between 0.5 and 1m have been recorded on some sites. Such a horizon does not therefore represent a turf line which developed over an abandoned site, or one uniform action over a wide area. By contrast, it must be interpreted as the product of varied and persistent activity over a dismantled settlement. On some sites in the City, such as that at Milk Street (Roskams 1978), the formation of the deposits began in the late 2nd to early 3rd century, while on some waterfront sites it occurred in the late 4th or early 5th century (Milne 1985, 33). Nevertheless, the discovery of Saxon pottery within the horizon shows that the dark grey silts were still being disturbed and added to several centuries later.

Pre-urban topography

The main topographical constraints that would have presented themselves to those concerned with the resettlement of the intra-mural area in the 9th to early 10th century were these: the line of the City wall itself, which, at that date, would have included at least some sections of the wall along the Thames waterfront; the River Thames, which flowed almost as far north as the line of present-day Thames Street; the River Walbrook, which, with several tributaries and attendant marshes, effectively divided the area in two; the precincts associated with such buildings as St Paul's minster which could be argued to be already within the walls; the major route-ways running across the area and aligned on gateways

107. Composite section showing the relationship of Buildings PEN2 *and* PEN3 *to the earliest surfacing of Botolph Lane. The underlying dumped deposits are shown as shaded (cf Figs 6, 108 (*PEN79*)).*

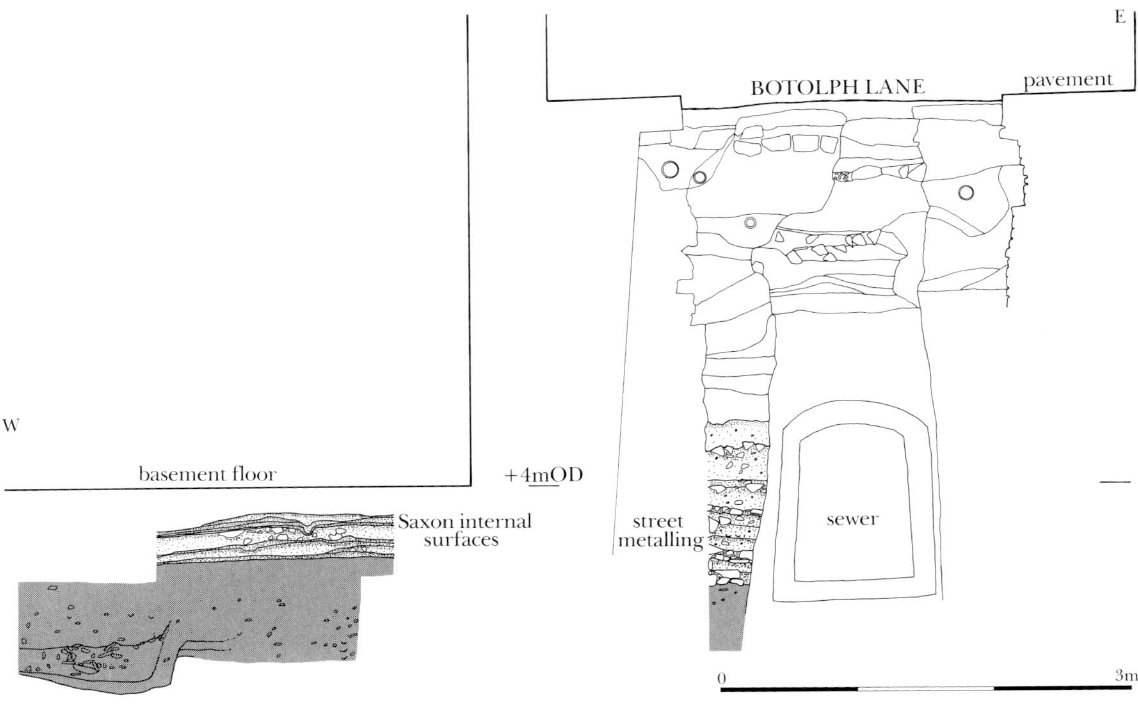

108. Section across Botolph Lane (A)*, showing the earliest street surface* (B)*, overlying a dump* (C)*, and laid at the same height as the internal Saxon floors* (D) *(cf Figs 6, 107* (PEN79)*)*.

in the town wall; and whatever other tracks, drove-roads, copses, meadowland, hedges, headlands or field boundaries may have been established over the remainder of the area. It was on that landscape that the new town had to be laid out. As a consequence of this, it might be expected that the street pattern that developed should reflect, however indirectly, the phase of land use it supplanted. Any observed regularity in that pattern might therefore be influenced as much by an underlying field system as by the superimposition of a carefully-surveyed grid.

Street development within the study areas

The earliest evidence of post-Roman structures takes the form of the sunken-featured buildings sealed within the dark grey silt horizon on both the Botolph Lane and Milk Street sites. Unfortunately, there was insufficient time or opportunity to do any more than observe these features during the contractor's earth-moving operations. However, their stratigraphic position perhaps hints at some isolated occupation of the intramural area before the major phase of re-settlement in the late 9th-early 10th century. It is not possible to say for certain whether any of these features are of sub-Roman or mid-Saxon date, or simply represent the very first phase of the Late Saxon activity.

Late 9th - 10th century: CP1

(Figs 4, 106-108)

In the waterfront study area, surface-laid buildings were built up against the Botolph Lane frontage and a truncated area was found up against Fish Street Hill free of pits but respected to the east by pits containing CP1 pottery. This implies that streets on the line of Fish Street Hill and Botolph Lane were established during this period. These two streets, both running northwards from the river bank at least as far as Eastcheap, (which is also assumed to date from this period) are therefore considered to be two of the primary thoroughfares in the resettled City. By contrast, the distribution of pits and features in the *c*.90m wide area between those streets shows that the predecessor of Pudding Lane was not a major street with a developed frontage in this period. However, at least one other street in the vicinity may have been established at the same time. That street is St Mary at Hill, which is some 100m to the east of Botolph Lane and, like that lane, its alignment continues north of Eastcheap, as Rood Lane.

A careful assessment of Saxon charters (Dyson 1978) has shown that streets running northwards from the waterfront in the Queenhithe area on the line of Huggin Hill and Little Trinity Lane were laid out in the late 9th century, as was an east-west street on the line of (Great) Trinity Lane (see Fig 109). It seems reasonable to assume that the same development would have seen some of the adjacent streets established. Immediately to the east lies Garlick Hill, the line of which, extended towards Cheapside, incorporates Bow Lane. The recent archaeological research has shown that a street approximately on the line of Bow Lane had been laid out by the late 9th to early 10th century. By this date, surface-laid buildings were laid up against its eastern edge at Well Court. Contemporary occupation on its western side is demonstrated by the presence of pits containing pottery of that date on the Watling Court site. Significantly those pits lie

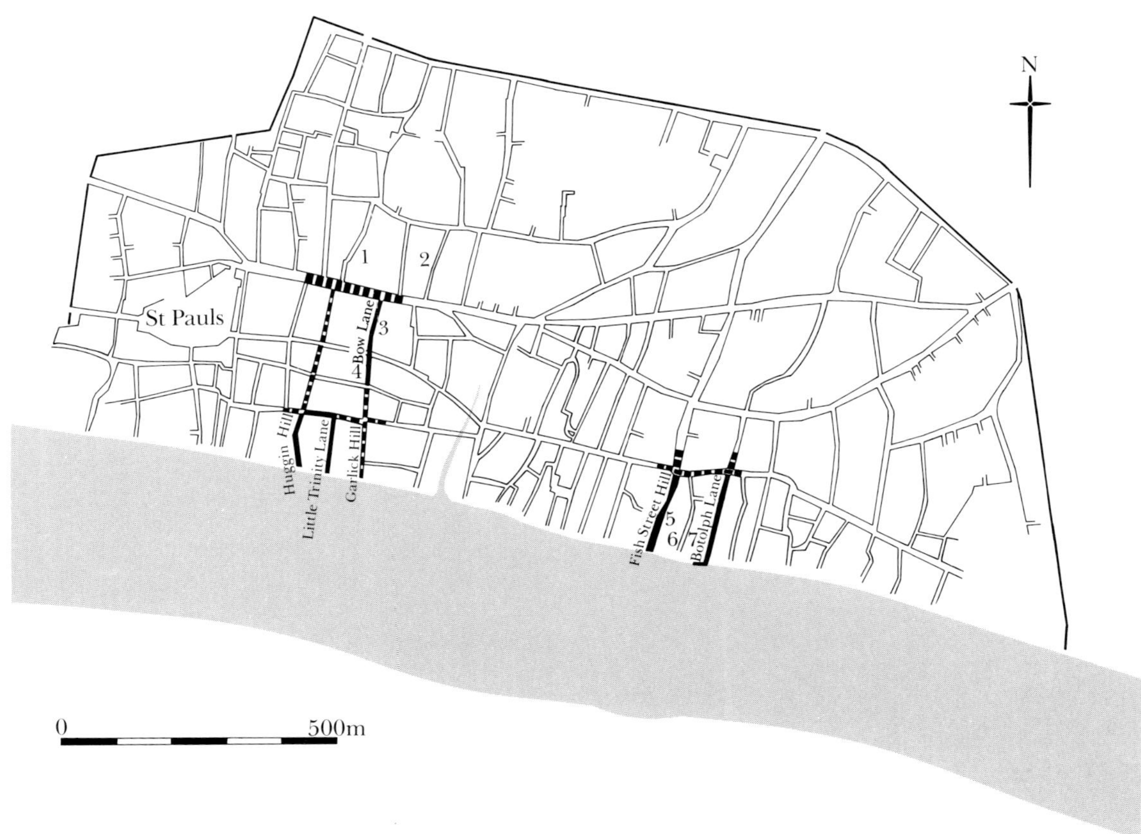

*109. Elements of the primary Saxon street grid in the study areas established in the 9th to early 10th century, superimposed upon the late medieval street plan. Streets known to be established at this date (*CP1-2*), are shown in black; other possible contemporary streets shown with a dashed line (cf Figs 110, 111): 1. Milk Street* MLK76; *2. Ironmonger Lane* IRO80; *3. Well Court* WEL79; *4. Watling Court* WAT78; *5. Fish Street Hill* FMO85; *6. Pudding Lane* PDN81; *7. Peninsular House* PEN79

west of a truncated but unpitted area against the edge of the street which may well have been occupied by surface-laid buildings. It is therefore possible to argue that the an early phase of Saxon redevelopment in the west of the City saw the introduction and occupation of a street grid incorporating north-south and east-west streets extending from the waterfront as far north as Cheapside (Westcheap).

However, the distribution of pits and other features on the Milk Street and Ironmonger Lane sites suggests that the street pattern north of Cheapside had not taken on its later form at this stage.

Mid-10th - 11th century: CP2

(Fig 109)

The pattern of development in the waterfront area remained much as in the previous phase. One notable addition was the introduction of the earliest structure in the sequence of buildings which were to occupy a property to the west of Pudding Lane, but not up against the frontage itself.

Immediately to the south of this study area lies the Billingsgate Lorry Park site (Fig 2), which was excavated in 1982-3. The detailed report on this important waterfront site will be published elsewhere, and all that will be noted here is that the earliest of the major riverside embankments features recorded on that site was erected during this rather than the preceeding phase. Its construction marks a significant development in the harbour area and its design took account of the foot of Botolph Lane, which already ran down onto the foreshore at that point.

110. Elements of the Saxon street grid in the study areas established in or by the 11th century (CP3-4). The area to the north of Cheapside and Eastcheap had been developed (cf Figs 109, 111).

In the area to the north of Cheapside, a more formal redevelopment took shape with the appearance of buildings erected up against the Milk Street frontage while all contemporary pits were dug well to the east. This suggests that the Milk Street alignment was established during this or early in the succeeding phase.

11th century: CP3-4

(Fig 110)

The general pattern remained the same within the study areas, although the development of individual properties and buildings underwent considerable change. It is worth noting that none of the large cellared buildings on the Watling Court site were set up against the street frontage. All may have been positioned at the rear of the principal ranges, which presumably incorporated surface-laid buildings at the front, the direct evidence of which was unfortunately truncated.

Neither the Pudding Lane nor the Ironmonger Lane frontage seem to have been extensively developed in this phase. However there was some evidence from a site excavated at 3-5 Bishopsgate in 1983 that at least the southern end of that road was established during this perod (Milne *et al* 1983). This is of importance to this study since it suggests that the street on the line of Fish Street Hill had almost certainly been settled north of Eastcheap (ie along what is now Gracechurch Street) at some earlier date. A bridge over the Thames must have been established at the southern end of Fish Street Hill by this date, although its exact position is not known.

12th century: CP 5-6

(Fig 111)

The main development in the study areas in this phase was the establishing of the Ironmonger

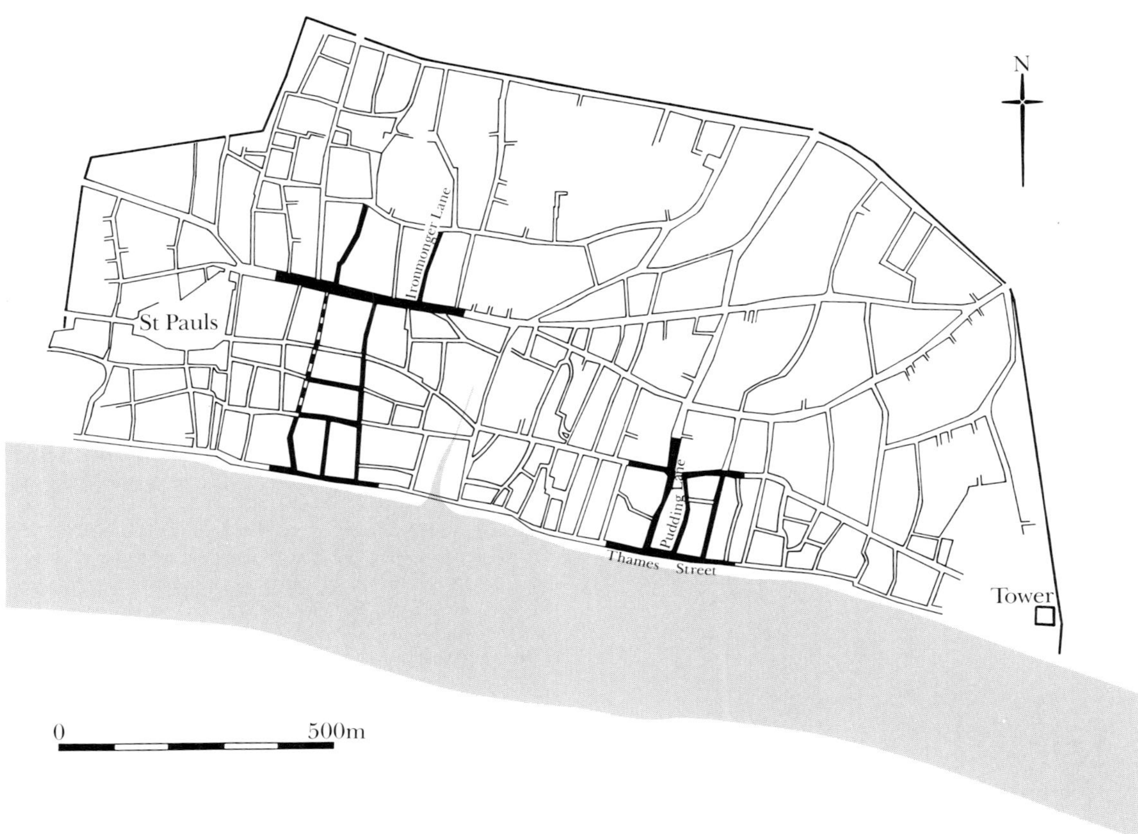

Lane and Pudding Lane streets as major thoroughfares. In both cases there was evidence to show that buildings were erected up against the frontage for the first time.

Summary and conclusions

In conclusion, it is suggested that certain large blocks of land between the River Thames and what later became Eastcheap and Cheapside were sub-divided in the late 9th and 10th century by a series of north-south streets. For example, Fish Street Hill, Bow Lane, and Botolph Lane and can all be dated to this period. The earliest documentary references to streets on these alignments are in the 12th, 13th and 14th centuries respectively (Ekwall 1954, 179, 80, 160). On the western side of the City, the larger grid thus formed also incorporated east-west streets such as Great Trinity Lane.

By the early 11th century, a subsequent phase of growth had seen the systematic settlement of at least one street to the north of Cheapside. Milk

111. Elements of the street grid in the study areas established in or by the 12th century (CP5). Some of the primary insulae have been subdivided (cf Figs 108, 110).

Street is the example examined in this report, the earliest historical reference to which is 12th century (Ekwall 1954, 76).

In the Billingsgate area, secondary properties were now established in the middle of the insulae, set well back from the primary frontage, as shown by Buildings PDN1-4 on the Pudding Lane site. Access to such secondary properties was presumably gained by a subsidiary back lane which ran between the rear boundaries of the primary properties. Such was the increase in population by the mid-12th century that this back lane was presumably realigned and up-graded, with the introduction of buildings laid out along the frontages of Pudding Lane. Lovat Lane, which lies just east of Botolph Lane, may have also developed in a similar way. The 13th and early 14th centuries saw another level of development within these insulae, with the development of buildings clustered around yards and courts behind both the primary and the secondary frontages described above. Some of these later additions to the street plan are shown on Fig 111 as lanes running east-west. This phase of street development in the Cheapside area is considered in more detail elsewhere (Schofield and Allen forthcoming).

Such a general pattern would be eloquent testimony to a rising population in the City during the Saxo-Norman period, and to one which sought accommodation in increasingly intensive nucleations around the main market streets and harbour areas. However, the study of the layout and subsequent sub-division of the original burgage plots is barely feasible on purely archaeological grounds at present.

The archaeological evidence presented in this report gives a clear picture of Saxo-Norman development within the study areas, with timber buildings set within an ordered framework of streets. It seems to be one of continued and significant expansion during this period, presumably reflecting rising prosperity. The Scandinavian and Norman sieges and conquests in the 11th century do not seem to have arrested growth in the long term, although the fire levels and waste plots recorded on the Botolph Lane sites show that the development of individual properties did not always run so smooth.

It remains to be seen how typical this pattern is for the City as a whole, and further research into this crucial period of London's history is clearly required. What can be said is that our understanding has certainly advanced since the 1960s, when the early medieval town was described as 'scattered groups of hovels laid out to no ordered plan' (Grimes 1968, 160). The new picture is the direct result of the application of open-area excavation techniques advocated by Professor Grimes as the only solution to the problem of understanding the medieval town: in his immortal phrase, 'Herein lies the justification for the pursuit of much unlovely detail' (Grimes 1968, 241).

BIBLIOGRAPHY

Addyman, P, 1972 The Anglo-Saxon house - a new review *Anglo-Saxon England*, **1**, 273-307

____, 1974 Excavations in York 1972-3 : first interim report *Antiq J*, **54**, 200-31

____, 1976 Excavations in York 1973-4 : second interim report, *Excavations in York Interim Reports*, **2**, CBA

____, 1979 Vernacular buildings below ground, *Archaeol J*, **136**, 69-75

____, 1980 The work of the York Archaeological Trust in 1980 Yorkshire Philosophical Society Ann Rep

Addyman, P, Goodall, I, *et al*; 1976 Norman church and door at Stillingfleet, North Yorks, *Archaeologia*, **106**, 75-105

Barker, P, 1977 *Techniques of Archaeological Excavation*

Barley, M (ed), 1976 *The Plans and Topography of Medieval Towns in England and Wales*, CBA Res Rep **14**

Barley, M (ed), 1977 *European Towns: their Archaeology and Early History*

Bateman, N, 1986 Bridgehead Revisited, *London Archaeol*, **5**, no 9, 233-41

Bateman, N, and Locker, A, 1982 The Sauce of the Thames *Lond Archaeol*, **4**, 8, 204-7

Bateman, N, and Milne, G, 1983 A Roman Harbour in London, *Britannia*, **14**, 207-26

Beresford, G, 1975 *The Medieval Clayland Village: Excavations at Goltho and Barton Blount*, Soc Med Archaeol monogr ser 6

____, 1977 The Excavation of a Moated House at Wingtringham, Huntingdonshire, *Archaeol J*, **134**, 194-286

____, 1979 Three Deserted Settlements on Dartmoor, *Medieval Archaeol*, **23**, 98-158

____, 1982 The Reconstruction of some Saxon Buildings at Goltho, Lincs, in Drury 1982, 113-23

Beresford, M, & Hurst, J, 1971 *Deserted Medieval Villages*

Biddle, M, 1976 Towns, in Wilson (ed) 1976, 99-150

Biddle, M & Hill, D, 1971 Late Saxon Planned Towns, *Antiq J*, **51**, 70-85

Biddle, M, Hudson, D, and Heighway, C, 1973 *The Future of London's Past*

Bishop, S, 1976 Skeldergate : Anglian and Anglo-Scandinavian Buildings in Addyman 1976, 14

Blanchard, L, 1980 Kirk Close— a Backland Excavation, in Turner Simpson & Stevenson (eds) 1980, 32-8

Bradley, R, Christie, J, & Johnston, D, 1966 *Forest Management Tables*, HMSO, Forestry Commission Booklet 16

Brisbane, M, forthcoming Excavations at Six Dials site

Brooke, C & Keir, G, 1975 *London 800-1216: the Shaping of a City*

Brunskill, R, 1971 *Illustrated Handbook of Vernacular Architecture*

Carver, M, 1979 Three Saxo Norman tenements in Durham City *Medieval Archaeol*, **23**, 1-80

Charles, F, 1982 The Construction of Buildings with Irregularly-spaced Posts, in Drury 1982, 101-12

Chew H M, & Kellaway W, 1973 *London Assize of Nuisance* 1301-1431, London Record Society, **10**

Chitwood, P, 1983 Excavations at 8 Telegraph Street, DUA Archive Report, MOL

Christie, H, Olsen, O, & Taylor, H, 1979 The Wooden Church of St Andrews at Greensted, Essex, *Antiq J*, **59**, 92-112

Clarke, H, 1984 *The Archaeology of Medieval England*

Crummy, P 1979 The system of measurement used in Town Planning from 9th to the 13th centuries in *Anglo-Saxon Studies in Archaeology and History*, BAR **72**, 149-64

Cunliffe, B, 1976 *Excavations at Portchester Castle, Vol II: Saxon* Soc Antiq Res Rep, **33**

Darrah, R, 1982 Working Unseasoned Oak, in McGrail (ed) 1982, 219-29

Davison, B, 1967 The Late Saxon town of Thetford: an interim report on the 1964-66 Excavations, *Medieval Archaeol*, **II**, 189-208

Drury, P (ed), 1982 *Structural Reconstruction: Approaches to the Interpretation of the Excavated Remains of Buildings*, BAR **110**

Dunmore, S, Loader, T, & Wade, K, 1976 Ipswich Archaeological Survey : 2nd interim report in West 1976, 135-140

Durham, B, 1977 Archaeological Investigations in St Aldates, Oxford, *Oxoniensia*, **42**, 83-203

——, 1980 Excavations at 9-11 St Martin's Street, Wallingford, *Oxford Archaeol Unit Ann Rep* 1980, 44-7

Dyer, C, 1986 English Peasant Houses in the later Middle Ages (1200-1500), *Medieval Archaeol*, **30**, 19-45

Dyson, T, 1978 Two Saxon land grants for Queenhithe, in *Collectanea Londoniensia*' ed J Bird, H Chapman & J Clark, London Middlesex Archaeol Soc Special Paper, **2**, 200-15

Dyson, T, & Schofield, J, 1984 Saxon London in J Haslam (ed) 1984, 285-313

Ekwall, E, 1954 *The Street Names of the City of London*

Geddes, J, 1982 The Construction of Medieval Doors, in McGrail 1982, 313-25

Graham-Campbell, J, & Kidd, D, 1980 *The Vikings*

Grimes, W, 1968 *The Excavation of Roman and Medieval London*

Hall, R, 1978 The Topography of Anglo-Scandinavian York, in R Hall (ed), *Viking-age York and the North*, CBA Res Rep **27**, 31-6

——, R, 1982 10th-century Woodworking in Coppergate, York, in McGrail 1982, 231-44

——, 1984a *The Excavations at York: the Viking Dig*

——, 1984b A Late Pre-Conquest Urban Building Tradition in P Addyman and V Black (eds), *Archaeological Papers from York Presented to M W Barley*, 71-77

——, 1986 Discussion in Moulden and Tweddle 1986

Haslam, J, (ed) 1984 *Anglo-Saxon Towns in Southern England*

Hassall, T, Durham, B, & Woods, H, 1974-5 Excavations at Oxford 1973-4 Sixth and Final Interim Report *Oxoniensia*, **39-40**, 53-61

Hauglid, R, 1976 *Norske Stavkirker: Bygningshistorisk Bakgrunn og Utvikling* (Oslo)

Herrnbrodt, A, 1958 *Der Husterknupp, eine Niederheinische Burlange des Fruhen Mittelalters* (Köln)

Hewett, C, 1969 *The Development of English Carpentry 1200 - 1700: an Essex Study*

——, 1980 *English Historic Carpentry*

——, 1982 Tool Marks on Surviving Works from the Saxon and Later Medieval Periods, in McGrail 1982, 339-48

Hobley, B and Schofield, J, 1977 Excavations in the City of London, First Interim Report, 1974-5, *Antiq J*, **57**, 31-66

Hodges, R, 1982 *Dark Age Economics: the Origins of Towns and Trade AD 600-1000*

Holdsworth, P, 1976 Saxon Southampton; a new review *Medieval Archaeol*, **20**, 26-61

——, 1980 *Excavation at Melbourne Street, Southampton, 1971-6*', CBA Res Rep 33

Hope-Taylor, B, 1977 *Yeavering : An Anglo-British centre of Northumbria*

Horsman, V, 1983 Saxon Buildings near Billingsgate, *Popular Archaeol*, **5**, no 4, 28-33

——, 1985 Rebuilding Saxon London, *Popular Archaeol*, **6**, no 12, 18-23

Huggins, P, 1976 The Excavation of an 11th-century Viking Hall and 14th-century Rooms at Waltham Abbey, Essex, 1969-71, *Medieval Archaeol*, **20**, 75-133

Huggins, P, Rodwell, K, & Rodwell, R, 1982 Anglo-Saxon and Scandinavian Building Measurements in Drury 1982, 21-65

Hurst, H, 1972, Excavations at Gloucester 1968-71: first interim report, *Antiq J*, **52**, 24-69

Hurst, J, 1979 *Excavations at Wharram Percy, North Yorkshire* 1950-60, Soc Medieval Archaeol monogr ser 8

Innocent, C, 1916 *The Development of English Building Construction*

James, S, Marshall, A, & Millett, M, 1984 An Early Medieval Building Tradition, *Archaeol J*, **141**, 182-215

Jones, D, 1980 *Excavations at Billingsgate Buildings 'Triangle', Lower Thames Street*, 1974, London Middlesex Archaeol Soc Special Paper, **4**

Jones, M, 1974 Excavations at Mucking Essex, 2nd interim report, *Antiq J*, **54**, 183-99

Jope, E, 1958 The Clarendon Hotel, Oxford Part 1 The Site, *Oxoniensia*, **23-4**, 1-83

King, A, 1979 Gauber High Pasture, Ribblehead—an interim report, in Hall 1979, 21-5

Marsden, P, Dyson, T, and Rhodes, M, 1975 Excavations on the Site of St Mildreds Church, Bread Street, London, 1973-4, *Trans London and Middlesex Archaeol Soc*, **26**, 171-207

McGrail, S, (ed), 1982 *Woodworking Techniques before AD 1500*, BAR Int Ser, **129**

Mason, D, 1985 *Excavations at Chester, 26-42 Lower Bridge Street 1974-6; the Dark Age and Saxon Periods*, Grosvenor Museum Archaeol Rep, **3**

Meeson, B, 1983 Plank-walled Building Technique and the Church of St Lawrence, Rushton Spencer, *Vernacular Architecture*, **14**, 29-35

Miller, L, 1977 New Fresh Wharf: 2, Saxon and Early Medieval Waterfronts, *London Archaeol*, **3**, no 2, 47-53

Milne, G, 1979 The Peasant Houses, in Hurst 1979, 67-73

____, 1980 Saxon Botolph Lane, *London Archaeol*, **3**, 423-30

____, 1982 Further Evidence for Roman London Bridge?, *Britannia* **13**, 271-86

____, 1985a *The Port of Roman London*

____, 1985b *The Archaeology of Medieval Waterfront Installations in London: a Structural, Comparative and Topographical Study* unpubl M Phil thesis, University of London

____, 1986 *The Great Fire of London*

Milne, G, Bateman, N, & Milne, C, 1983 Bank Deposits with Interest, *London Archaeol*, **4**, no 15, 395-400

Milne, G & Milne, C, 1985, A Building in Pudding Lane burnt in the Great Fire of 1666, *Trans London Middlesex Archaeol Soc*, **36**, 169-82

Morris, J, (ed), 1975 *Domesday Book: 3, Surrey*

Moulden, J, & Tweddle, D, 1986 *Anglo-Scandinavian Settlement South-west of the Ouse*, (The Archaeology of York, **8/4**)

Murray, H, 1980 Medieval Wooden and Wattle Buildings Excavated in Perth and Aberdeen in Turner, Simpson & Stevenson (ed) 1980, 39-49

____, *1983 Viking Buildings in Dublin* BAR **119**

Norton, J, 1982 Ironmonger Lane *London Archaeol*, **4**, 7, 171-6

Oswald, O, 1962-3 Excavation of a 13th-century Wooden Building at Weoley Castle, Birmingham, *Medieval Archaeol*, **6-7**, 109-34

Perring, D, 1981 *Early Medieval Occupation at Flaxengate, Lincoln* (The Archaeology of Lincoln, **IX.1**)

____, 1982 Excavations at Watling Court: Part 2 *London Archaeol*, **4**, no 8, 208-13

Rackham, O, 1976 *Trees and Woodland in the British Landscape*

____, 1982 The Growing and Transport of Timbers and Underwood in McGrail (ed) 1982, 199-218

Radley, J, 1971 Economic Aspects of Anglo-Danish York *Medieval Archaeol*, **15**, 37-57

Rahtz, P, & Sheridan, K, 1972 Fifth Report of Excavations at Tamworth, Staffs, 1971. A Saxon Watermill in Bolebridge Street, *Trans S Staffordshire Archaeol & Hist Soc*, **13**, 9-16

Rahtz, P, 1976 Buildings and Rural Settlement in Wilson (ed) 1976, 49-98: and also Gazetteer, 405-52

____, 1979 *The Saxon and Medieval Palaces at Cheddar*, BAR **65**

Rodwell, W, 1976 The Archaeological Investigation of Hadstock Church, Essex: An Interim Report, *Antiq J*, **56**, 55-71

Roskams, S, 1978 The Milk Street Excavations: 1, *London Archaeol*, **3**, no 8, 199-205

Roskams, S & Schofield, J, 1978 The Milk Street Excavation: Part 2 *London Archaeol*, **3**, no 9, 227-34

Schmidt, H, 1973 The Trelleborg House Reconsidered *Medieval Archaeol* **17**, 52-77

Schofield, J, 1975 Seal House, *London Archaeol*, **49**, 54-57

____, 1984 *The Building of London from the Conquest to the Great Fire*

Schofield, J, & Allen, P, forthcoming *Medieval property development in the area of Cheapside*

Smith, J T, 1982 The Validity of Inference from Archaeological Evidence, in Drury (ed) 1982, 7-19

Stead, I, 1966-9 An Excavation at King's Square, York, 1957, *Yorks Archaeol J*, **42**, 151-68

Tatton-Brown, T, 1986, The Topography of Anglo-Saxon London, *Antiquity*, **60**, 21-8

Thompson, A, 1976 GPO Newgate Street, *London Archaeol*, **2**, no 15, 400-1

Thompson, M, 1967 *Novgorod the Great*

Turner Simpson, A, & Stevenson, S, (ed) 1980 *Town Houses and Structures in Medieval Scotland: A Seminar*, Scottish Burgh Survey

Vince, A (ed) forthcoming, *Aspects of Saxo-Norman London*, Vol II, *Finds and environmental evidence*

Wallace, P, 1982 Carpentry in Ireland, AD 900-1300: the Wood Quay Evidence, in McGrail 1982, 263-99

Webster, L, & Cherry, J, 1980 Medieval Britain in 1979 *Medieval Archaeol*, **24**, 218-64

West, S, 1969 The Anglo-Saxon Village of West Stow: an interim report of the excavations 1965-8, *Medieval Archaeol*, **13**, 1-20

——, 1985 *West Stow: the Anglo-Saxon village*, East Anglian Archaeol Rep **24**

Wheeler, R, 1935 *London and the Saxons* London Museum Cat 6

Williams, J & Shaw, 1981, Excavations in Chalk Lane, Northampton 1975-8, *Northamptonshire Archaeol*, **16**, 87-135

Wilson, D, (ed) 1976 *The Archaeology of Anglo-Saxon England*

Youngs, S, Clark, J, & Barry, T, 1985 Medieval Britain and Ireland in 1984 *Medieval Archaeol*, **29**, 158-230

ACKNOWLEDGEMENTS

An archaeological study such as this one, which deals with several sites excavated over a decade, builds on the fieldwork, skills, advice and ideas of far too many people to mention all by name. Credit must be paid to all the archaeologists, both volunteers and professionals, whose hard work on the Saxon levels of the seven sites is considered in this volume. Without their careful record, there could be no subsequent study. In particular, N Bateman, M Burch, I Blair, D Bowler, J Burke-Easton, G Cadman, P Cardiff, C Guy, R Harris, J Harrison, V de Hoog, W Horton, A Isaacs, M Inzani, N Inzani, M Lee, T Mackinder, J Milner, J Norton, D Perring, P Roberts, M Samuel, C Unwin, L Walker and P Thompsons's dedicated CoLAS team all made valuable contributions.

Information and advice has also been gratefully received from T Dyson and many other colleagues in the Museum of London, as well as from Marion Blockley (Clwyd-Powys Archaeological Trust), Carolyn Dallas (Norfolk Archaeological Unit), Dr Patrick Wallace (National Museum of Ireland), but particularly from Dr Richard Hall (York Archaeological Trust). However, errors which remain in this report are the responsibility of its authors.

Generous financial support for the excavations, research and publication came from a variety of sources, including City of London Archaeological Trust, English Property Corporation, Guardian Royal Exchange, Manpower Services Commission, National Provident Institution, Speyhawk, Verronworth & Vitiglade, Wates Development and also from the Historic Buildings & Monuments Commission (formerly the Department of Environment) through the good offices of G Andrews, B Davison and G Chitty. Access to the sites was negotiated by B Hobley and J Schofield, who also organised the excavations (with the exception of Fish Street Hill, organised by J Maloney).

The photography is principally the work of J Bailey, T Hurst and J Scrivener, with the exception of Fig 99 which is published by kind permission of the York Archaeological Trust. The reconstruction of a street scene in Saxo-Norman London (on the front cover) was painted by John Pearson, and the rest of the illustrations are by Christine Milne. For translations of the Summary we thank Dominique de Moulins and Friederike Hammer.

SUMMARIES IN FRENCH AND GERMAN

Résumé

Ce volume est le premier d'une série qui réexaminera le développement de Londres à l'époque saxo-normande. Il se base sur les témoignages archéologiques provenant de sept sites fouillés entre 1976 et 1985 dans les environs de Billingsgate et de Cheapside dans la Cité de Londres. Il y a peu de traces d'occupation pendant la période saxonne moyenne sur ces sites car il semble qu'alors le centre d'occupation principal se trouvait à l'ouest de la ville romaine dans ce qui est maintenant le quartier de Aldwich et du Strand. Les sept sites ont pris une importance grandissante à partir de la periode saxonne tardive.

Dans les deux premières parties de ce volume, on a expliqué les circonstances dans lesquelles le projet a pris place et les méthodes de datation employées; on y a aussi fait le résumé des résultats obtenus pour chaque fouille. Dans les sections 3 a 6, on a catalogué décrit et analysé les restes souvent fragmentés d' environ 50 bâtiments saxons et normands.

L'étude détaillée de ce matériel souvent mal préservé a mis en évidence différents types de bâtiments et de traditions et techniques de construction. Trois types principaux de structures sont présents; on a examiné les caractéristiques et fonctions probables de chacun de ces types. Il semble que les bâtiments à un seul étage sans fondation représentent les structures d'habitation type; ils sont placés directement le long de la rue. Les structures à sol enfoui représentent les dépendances ou les huttes de stockage que l'on trouve d'habitude dans la cour derrière le bâtiment principal. Les bâtiments avec sous-sols sont un type urbain de structures unique dans lequel la partie en sous-sol était placée en-dessous ou derrière le bâtiment lui-même.

La grande variété de techniques de construction que l'on a pu observer comprend l'utilisation de poteaux, de piquets, de clayonnage et de murs fixés sur des poutres de soubassement. Dans la section 7 on a également documenté les sols, les porte, les foyers et les fours et on a fait la reconstruction de deux bâtiments-type.

De plus, les fouilles ont permis de révéler l'origine d'une partie du plan en quadrillage de la Cité à travers l'étude des rues elles-même et la disposition des maisons qui leur sont associées . On a avancé, dans la section 8, l'idée que les rues médievales situées juste au nord de Billingsgate n'ont pas été construites d'un seul coup au 9ème–10ème siècle, mais sont le résultat d'un développement graduel durant lequel les rues principales et secondaires peuvent être distinguées.

Les rapports détaillés sur la céramique et les autres objets provenant des sites dont il est question ici se trouvent dans le volume faisant paire avec celui-ci et s'intitule *Aspects of Saxo-Norman London, Volume II: Finds and Environmental Evidence* (Traits de Londres Saxo-Normand, volume II: Objets et Environnement), édité par Alan Vince.

Zusammenfassung

Dieser erste Band einer größeren Neuerfassung der Entwicklung des sächsisch-normannischen Londons beruht auf den Fakten der sieben Ausgrabungen zwischen 1976 und 1985 in den Gegenden um Cheapside und Billingsgate in der City von London. Nur wenige Anzeichen von Bebauung reichen hier in die mittlere Sachsenzeit zurück, da das Zentrum der Siedlung westlich der römischen Stadtmauer, in der Aldwich-Strand Gegend lag. Alle sieben Ausgrabungen der City zeugen von umfangreicher Bauentwicklung seit der späten Sachsenzeit.

Im ersten und zweiten Teil dieses Bandes werden der Hintergrund des Projektes und die Datierungsmethoden erläutert, außerdem sind hier die Resultate der einzelnen Ausgrabungen zusammengefaßt. Im Teil 3–6 sind die oft bruchstückhaften überreste von ungefähr 50 sächsisch-normannischen Bauten katalogisiert, beschrieben und untersucht.

Das Studium der Einzelheiten des oft schlecht überkommenen Materials zeigt dennoch verschiedene Bauweisen, Traditionen und Techniken. Drei Hauptarten von Gebäuden sind vertreten und ihre Merkmale und mögliche Funktionen werden erwogen. Die einstöckigen ebenerdigen Gebäude scheinen die verbreitetste Art der Wohnhäuser gewesen zu sein, die direkt an die Straßenfront gebaut waren. Strukturen, deren Fußböden unter der Erdoberfläche lagen, befanden sich meistens in Höfen hinter den Gebäuden und wurden zur Lagerung von Waren benutzt, während der integrierte Keller ein rein städtisches Element der Bauweise war, in dem der unterirdische Teil unter oder hinter dem Hauptgebäude lag.

Die verschiedenen Bautechniken der Häuserwände bestanden unter anderem aus in die Erde getriebenen Pfosten oder Sprossen, Flecht-und Fachwerk, und aus Wänden die über Holzplankenfundamenten errichtet waren. Außerdem sind die Vorkommen der Fußböden, Herde und öfen besprochen, und in Teil 7 werden Rekonstruktionen von zwei Haustypen vorgeschlagen.

Außerdem wurden durch die Ausgrabungen der Straßen selbst Teile der Anfänge des neuen Straßensystems und der Aufteilung der angrenzenden Grundstücke in der City gefunden. Dabei wird in Teil 8 gezeigt, daß die mittelalterlichen Straßen im Norden von Billingsgate nicht in einter Phase im 9.–10. Jahrhundert ausgelegt wurden, sondern daß sie Teil einer langsamen Entwicklung waren, in der frühere und spätere Straßen unterschieden werden können.

Die ausführliche Auseinandersetzung mit den Funden der Ausgrabungen befindet sich im zweiten Band, *Aspects of Saxo-Norman London, Volume II: Finds and Environmental Evidence*, herausgegeben von Alan Vince.